Rethinking International Political Economy

RETHINKING POLITICAL SCIENCE AND INTERNATIONAL STUDIES

This series is a forum for innovative scholarly writing from across all substantive fields of political science and international studies. The series aims to enrich the study of these fields by promoting a cutting-edge approach to thought and analysis. Academic scrutiny and challenge is an essential component in the development of political science and international studies as fields of study, and the act of re-thinking and re-examining principles and precepts that may have been long-held is imperative.

Rethinking Political Science and International Studies showcases authored books that address the field from a new angle, expose the weaknesses of existing concepts and arguments, or 're-frame' the topic in some way. This might be through the introduction of radical ideas, through the integration of perspectives from other fields or even disciplines, through challenging existing paradigms, or simply through a level of analysis that elevates or sharpens our understanding of a subject.

Titles in the series include:

Rethinking International Relations
Bertrand Badie

Rethinking International Political Economy
Benjamin J. Cohen

Rethinking International Political Economy

Benjamin J. Cohen

Distinguished Professor Emeritus, Department of Political Science, University of California, Santa Barbara, USA

RETHINKING POLITICAL SCIENCE AND
INTERNATIONAL STUDIES

Edward Elgar
PUBLISHING

Cheltenham, UK • Northampton, MA, USA

Published by
Edward Elgar Publishing Limited
The Lypiatts
15 Lansdown Road
Cheltenham
Glos GL50 2JA
UK

Edward Elgar Publishing, Inc.
William Pratt House
9 Dewey Court
Northampton
Massachusetts 01060
USA

Paperback edition 2023

A catalogue record for this book
is available from the British Library

Library of Congress Control Number: 2022931091

This book is available electronically in the **Elgar**online
Political Science and Public Policy subject collection
http://dx.doi.org/10.4337/9781789908657

ISBN 978 1 78990 864 0 (cased)
ISBN 978 1 78990 865 7 (eBook)
ISBN 978 1 0353 1343 3 (paperback)

Printed and bound by CPI Group (UK) Ltd, Croydon, CR0 4YY

For the memory of Peter Kenen and Charlie Kindleberger,
one tall, one short, both giants

"Words ought to be a little wild, for they are the assault of thoughts on
the unthinking."
– John Maynard Keynes

Contents

Preface and acknowledgments

I did not begin my professional life under the banner of International Political Economy (IPE). All of my formal university training, way back in the dimly remembered past, was in conventional economics – a much more prosaic choice. I knew from the start of my studies that I wanted to specialize in economics. More to the point, I wanted to specialize in *international* economics. As I have often joked to my students, I wanted to see as much of the world as possible; and of all the branches of the economics discipline, international economics seemed to promise the greatest opportunity for travel. At the time I had never even heard of something called political economy. It was only after I took my first academic post, nearly six decades ago, that I began to broaden my ambitions to encompass not just the economics but also the politics of international affairs. An odyssey had begun. It has been a most satisfying journey.

My transition to IPE did not take place quickly. How could I convert to something that did not even yet exist as a recognized field of study? There were of course versions of IPE to be found at the time in Latin America and elsewhere in the developing world, in the writings of Marxists and others of a more critical persuasion. Scholars like these had little difficulty seeing connections between economics and politics in the global capitalist system. But in the Western social science canon in which I was trained, there was as yet no formal disciplinary home for what today we call political economy. The established disciplines of political science and economics had long been firmly separated, with hardly a word passed between them. There was certainly no regular communication between them about international affairs. I recall that in the one political science course that I took as an undergraduate, an introduction to world politics, there was rarely any mention at all of the "low politics" of economic relations; the lectures were all about military security and the threat of nuclear weapons. Conversely, in none of my many economics courses did I ever hear anything about political processes or institutions; classes were all about resource efficiency, market stabilization, and the elusive hunt for Pareto optimality. The twain never met.

But I was lucky. As it turned out, I was not alone. In the late 1960s and early 1970s, a pioneering generation of scholars on the two sides of the Atlantic was just starting to explore the diverse political dimensions of the world economy. These included giants like Bob Gilpin, Peter Katzenstein, Bob Keohane, Charlie Kindleberger, and Susan Strange. A new field of study called International Political Economy was beginning to emerge (or, as some would have it, re-emerge).

Until exposed to pioneering efforts like those, my own career path remained unremarkable. I studied conventional international economics under the tutelage of Peter Kenen, one of the top international economists of the day. Then, with my new doctorate in hand, I worked for two years as a research economist at the Federal Reserve Bank of New York; and even after beginning my teaching career at Princeton University in 1964, I continued to stick to the standards of orthodox economics. A turning point came in 1968, when I arrived in London to spend a sabbatical year writing a book on the British pound sterling (Cohen 1971). If you're going to research the pound, I was told, I must meet Strange, who at the time was also working on a book on sterling – published not long after under the title *Sterling and British Policy* (Strange 1971). So I sought her out. When we got together, I dutifully told her about my plan to do a strictly economic cost–benefit calculus of sterling's role as an international currency. "Oh, Jerry," Susan replied, squinting at me through hooded eyes, "you can't possibly write about the pound without talking about the politics, too" – a remonstration that she would subsequently repeat to me on every possible occasion. At the time I resisted, with a stubbornness born of my conventional economics training. The loss was mine. Her book, a monumental study, turned out to be far more interesting.

Ultimately, Strange's message did get through. By the time I got back to the United States, I was determined – thanks, in good part, to her – to dip my toe into this alluring new current of scholarship. In quick order that led me to produce two eager sallies into the emerging field. The first was *The Question of Imperialism: The Political Economy of Dominance and Dependence* (1973), written largely in response to persistent queries from my students about the seeming inequities of the global economic system. The second was a successor to my sterling book, *Organizing the World's Money* (Cohen 1977), which may legitimately be described as the first fully integrated exploration of the economic and political dimensions of global monetary governance. These two works marked the completion of my intellectual transformation – "one of the rare cases of an economist," one observer wrote of me, "who came in from the cold of the dismal science" (Underhill 2000: 811). Ever since, IPE has been my scholarly home.

Over time, however, the home provided to me by IPE seems to have fallen increasingly into disrepair. Not everyone will agree, of course. For many in the field, IPE is thriving as never before. But I dissent. Over the years, I have tried to learn as much as I could about the field, both its strengths and its weaknesses. Unlike a good number of my American colleagues, I have also made a determined effort to inform myself about versions of IPE to be found in other parts of the world – not just locally in the United States, where I happened to study – and have even written about them.

First came *International Political Economy: An Intellectual History* (Cohen 2008), in which I sought to provide a brief history of the field since the late 1960s. The coverage of that volume was deliberately limited to the English-speaking world – otherwise known as the "Anglosphere" – defined here to include mainly the United States, Canada, the British Isles, and the Antipodes. It was also limited to what might be considered mainstream conceptions of IPE in the Anglosphere, excluding heterodox outliers. Though my intention was to broaden horizons by going beyond a single orthodoxy, I was surprised to find the book criticized for being, if anything, unduly narrow in its coverage. In the words of one commentary, "Cohen's account excludes too much ... These exclusions amount to omitting a considerable part of what is taught and written in IPE" (Leander 2009: 322–3). Upon reflection, I found I had to agree. Hence a few years later I produced a second book, *Advanced Introduction to International Political Economy*, now in its second edition (Cohen 2019), which may be considered as something of a sequel to my earlier *Intellectual History*. *Advanced Introduction* took us much further afield, broadening perspectives even more. My aim in that volume was to provide a comprehensive *tour d'horizon* of IPE as it exists across the globe.

Regrettably, though, the more I have learned about IPE in its many guises, the more unhappy I find myself with what our area of inquiry has gradually become. Some may feel that is simply because I have grown old and cranky. There could be some truth to that. (My wife, for one, might heartily concur.) Others will accuse me of pessimism, perhaps even dank paranoia. But mine is not a *cri de coeur* of despair. I am more inclined to see myself as offering a bit of light, a realistic way forward, at a moment of gathering darkness.

To be blunt: I am convinced that our train has gone off its tracks, moving in directions that are misguided if not absolutely mindless. Pathologies beset the field that could threaten its vitality, even its very existence. Starting with an essay published in 2007, "The Transatlantic Divide: Why are American and British IPE So Different?" (Cohen 2007) and continuing with my *Intellectual History* and *Advanced Introduction* and a slew of articles, I have mounted a long-running campaign to persuade my scholarly colleagues to open their minds to reconsider the substance and purpose of what we do – in short, to rethink IPE. This book continues that effort.

Rethinking International Political Economy summarizes in comprehensive fashion my judgment of where the field of IPE has gone wrong and where it should instead be heading. The title is not meant to suggest that we must wipe the slate clean and start over. There is much of value in the field that can and should be preserved. Nor does it mean rewinding to some purported Golden Age. There never was such a thing. Rethinking means building on what has already been accomplished while making course corrections where needed. It is not too late to save IPE from itself.

But will anyone listen? Back when I was just getting started on this project, a well-established senior colleague advised me to stop wasting my time. His intentions were honorable. No one will care, he warned. Minds are already made up and are unlikely to be amenable to revision. Too much time and effort have been invested in the status quo. I know from bitter experience that my kind friend could be right. There are indeed many in the field who see no reason at all for significant change. Once, after I explained some of my ideas, another eminent colleague responded, "Get serious, Jerry." Well, I *am* serious, and I like to think that there are also many fellow scholars who might share my concerns. I can only hope that my arguments here will be given a fair hearing.

My intended audience comprises two groups in particular. First are my scholarly peers in universities and research institutions around the world, whose interests encompass or border on some aspect of IPE. These are the people who, by their publications, teaching, and other professional activities, collectively define the parameters of the field as it exists today. And second are the many students of IPE in classrooms across the globe. These are the souls who will define the field as it will be practiced tomorrow. Modestly, my ambition is to change minds in the first group and to help shape minds in the second. I make no secret of my desire to shake things up a bit. My aim is to be disruptive – but also constructive.

*****

A book like this would hardly have been possible without the generous help and encouragement of a large number of friends and colleagues, though of course none of them can be held responsible for anything that I say here. I am indebted to them all for their support.

I am especially grateful to seven friends who kindly consented to read the entire manuscript of this book while it was still in preparation, providing valuable critiques. These were Greg Chin, Bob Denemark, Randy Germain, Jeremy Green, Andrew Walter, Hongying Wang, and Matthew Watson. I am also deeply indebted to others who read one or more of the chapters in draft, including Jeff Chwieroth, Miles Kahler, Peter Katzenstein, Bob Keohane, David Lake, Matthias Matthijs, Craig Murphy, and Kevin Young.

These friends and a substantial number of other colleagues also graciously consented to respond to my efforts when this project was just getting under way to solicit their views on the issues I intended to address. In all, some 54 fellow scholars shared their thoughts with me – a broad cross-section of the discipline including both junior and senior researchers and representing a range of nationalities and theoretical orientations. At various points in the text some of these colleagues are quoted. But their words are offered without attribution in an effort to safeguard their anonymity. In all such cases, comments and observations are reproduced faithfully from private communications. These Good Samaritans include Leslie Armijo, David Bearce, Jacqueline Best, Steve Best, Mark Blyth, Lawrence Broz, Christopher Chase-Dunn, Stephen Chaudoin, Jeff Chwieroth, Bob Denemark, Jeff Frieden, Randy Germain, Jeremy Green, Mark Hallerberg, Shahar Hameiri, Eric Helleiner, Randy Henning, Nicolas Jabko, Joe Jupille, Miles Kahler, Saori Katada, Peter Katzenstein, Ryan Katz-Rosene, Bob Keohane, Jonathan Kirshner, David Lake, David Leblang, Ed Manfield, Matthias Matthijs, Dan McDowell, Kate McNamara, Daniel Mügge, Craig Murphy, Andreas Nölke, Robert O'Brien, Miguel Otero-Iglesias, Lou Pauly, Tom Pepinsky, Lucia Quaglia, Thomas Risse, Bill Robinson, Nita Rudra, Mark Schwartz, Ben Selwyn, Jason Sharman, Tim Sinclair, David Steinberg, Federico Steinberg, Geoffrey Underhill, Andrew Walter, Hongying Wang, Matthew Watson, Wil Winecoff, and Kevin Young.

Portions of this manuscript were presented and discussed in colloquia at Waterloo University (Canada) and FLACSO Quito (Ecuador). The comments and suggestions I received from participants at these events were especially valuable. Useful observations also came from two students in the Global Studies program at the University of California Santa Barbara, Brett Aho and Mariah Miller.

In addition, I benefitted greatly from the research assistance of several of my students in the UCSB Political Science Department, including Vashnishtha Doshi, Andrew Johnson, Eric Stein, Ingmar Sturm, and Annjulie Vester. Their industrious support is also gratefully acknowledged.

This book is dedicated to the memory of Peter Kenen and Charlie Kindleberger, two giants of the economics profession whose intellect and ideas have inspired me for more than half a century.

Finally, my sincere thanks go to anyone out there who does actually bother to read what I have to say in the following pages. You will find that my tone is provocative. That is deliberate. Though I do not mean to be shrilly polemical, I do hope to shake people out of their comfort zone. A little iconoclasm can go a long way.

BJC

REFERENCES

Cohen, Benjamin J. (1971), *The Future of Sterling as an International Currency* (London: Macmillan).

Cohen, Benjamin J. (1973), *The Question of Imperialism: The Political Economy of Dominance and Dependence* (New York: Basic Books).

Cohen, Benjamin J. (1977), *Organizing the World's Money: The Political Economy of International Monetary Relations* (New York: Basic Books).

Cohen, Benjamin J. (2007), "The Transatlantic Divide: Why are American and British IPE So Different?" *Review of International Political Economy* 14:2, 197–219.

Cohen, Benjamin J. (2008), *International Political Economy: An Intellectual History* (Princeton, NJ: Princeton University Press).

Cohen, Benjamin J. (2019), *Advanced Introduction to International Political Economy*, revised 2nd edition (Cheltenham, UK and Northampton, MA, USA: Edward Elgar Publishing).

Leander, Anna (2009), "Why We Need Multiple Stories about the Global Political Economy," *Review of International Political Economy* 16:2, 321–8.

Strange, Susan (1971), *Sterling and British Policy: A Political Study of an International Currency in Decline* (London: Oxford University Press).

Underhill, Geoffrey R.D. (2000), "State, Market, and Global Political Economy: Genealogy of an (Inter?) Discipline," *International Affairs* 76:4, 805–24.

Abbreviations

BISA	British International Studies Association
CHPE	Comparative Historical Political Economy
CMB	Cosmic Microwave Background
EIPE	Everyday International Political Economy
GEPE	Global Ecological Political Economy
GFC	Global Financial Crisis
GPE	Global Political Economy
HIPE	Historical International Political Economy
IO	*International Organization*
IPE	International Political Economy
IPEG	International Political Economy Group
IPES	International Political Economy Society
IR	International Relations
ISA	International Studies Association
ISQ	*International Studies Quarterly*
NPE	*New Political Economy*
OEP	Open Economy Politics
PECI	Political Economy of Complex Interdependence
PRC	People's Republic of China
REF	Research Excellence Framework
RIPE	*Review of International Political Economy*
RMP	Rate My Professors (website)
SPERI	Sheffield Political Economy Research Institute
TRIP	Teaching, Research and International Policy (project)
UK	United Kingdom
US	United States

1. Introduction

It is time to rethink International Political Economy. Now a widely recognized area of scholarly inquiry, the modern field of International Political Economy (IPE) has blossomed for more than half a century (though its roots, of course, go much further back). But half a dozen decades are more than enough time for an academic field of study to develop critical, not to say existential, pathologies. Today the field seems to have fallen victim to a range of serious maladies.

Signs of disaffection are sprouting, in conversation and correspondence if not (yet) much in print. (Most colleagues, I find, are more willing to express their concerns in private than in public.) Many worry about the field's future. Tellingly, a prominent IPE scholar mentioned to me recently that a departmental colleague had just asked him, not at all in jest, "IPE was once an important field, wasn't it?" The implication, of course, was that now the field has gone into sad decline. Has IPE passed its peak?

Specialists can of course take great pride in modern IPE's many achievements, which are undeniable. The field did indeed become important. But we also need to face up to an onslaught of accumulating deficiencies, which if not addressed could fatally imperil the field's future standing. IPE is hardly the first academic specialty to suffer something like a debilitating mid-life crisis; there is nothing unique about the field in that respect. Most areas of scholarly inquiry become introspective from time to time. But in IPE today unhealthy symptoms seem particularly acute. Over the years our specialty has seemingly switched to autopilot, taking things for granted and drifting heedlessly off course. More and more, a once-vibrant field seems to be merely sleepwalking its way through life. A wake-up call is needed.

Where has IPE gone wrong? The field's incipient failings can be grouped into two clusters. One cluster includes deficiencies that are common to the field as a whole. The other encompasses issues that are hotly debated within the frontiers of the field. These can be called, respectively, IPE's *joint* problems and its *divisive* problems. All of them may be regarded as pathologies, in the sense that they represent deviations from what could be considered robust good health. Though often mutually reinforcing, they are each quite distinctive in the way they threaten the well-being of the field. Each will be introduced briefly in this chapter, setting the stage for the broader analysis to follow.

DIVERSITY

I begin with a deceptively simple question: What is International Political Economy? The question has no simple answer.

Without capital letters, international political economy is generally understood to refer to the material world around us – the myriad connections between economics and politics in everyday life. But that is not our subject here, at least not directly. Our subject is the academic field that gives meaning to those connections, by interpreting evidence and offering insight. Standard practice distinguishes our subject from the material world by using the capitalized words International Political Economy to stand for the field of study. That will be my practice here as well. Our interest is in IPE understood as an area of intellectual inquiry.

Among possible definitions, my personal favorite comes from Robert Gilpin, one of the pioneers of IPE in the United States. International Political Economy, he suggested, may be thought of as "the reciprocal and dynamic interaction in international relations of the pursuit of wealth and the pursuit of power" (Gilpin 1975: 43). By pursuit of wealth, Gilpin had in mind the realm of economics: the role of markets and other allocative mechanisms and the challenges of providing for material welfare, which are among the central concerns of economists. By pursuit of power, he had in mind the realm of politics: the role of the state and other political actors and the challenges of effective governance, which are among the central concerns of political scientists. By international relations he meant actions and outcomes that extend across national frontiers, which are among the central concerns of students of global affairs. By reciprocal he meant that neither economics nor politics takes precedence: each influences and, in turn, is impacted by the other. And by dynamic he meant that nothing can be taken for granted: things change. To a remarkable degree, this concise definition captures what the field is all about. For me, it represents the irreducible core of what we mean by IPE.

Beyond that core, however, perspectives diverge. Scholars may agree on the basics suggested by Gilpin. IPE is seen to be a multidisciplinary (or interdisciplinary) area of inquiry that has something to do with economics ("pursuit of wealth"), something to do with politics ("pursuit of power"), something to do with the world beyond the confines of a single sovereign state ("international relations"), and something to do with interactions that are both complex ("reciprocal") and mutable ("dynamic"). But that is about as far as consensus goes. Beyond that high level of generalization, definitions vary widely in their specifics. In practical terms, there seem to be almost as many visions of IPE as there are specialists in the subject – effectively, many variations on a few basic themes. Diversity rules.

Diversity of perspectives, of course, should not be confused with diversity of personnel. In popular parlance, diversity is often used to refer to variance in the attributes of individuals in a population of some kind – personal characteristics such as gender, race, religion, or ethnicity. Here, however, it is the variance among visions that is at issue, not variance among individuals. The diversity we are addressing is intellectual and has to do with thought processes: the differences among alternative understandings of what our field of study should look like. Beyond IPE's irreducible core, these differences can be enormous. The point is well made by the ancient Indian parable of the blind men and the elephant:

> A group of blind men heard that a strange animal, called an elephant, had been brought to the town, but none of them were aware of its shape and form. Out of curiosity, they said: "We must inspect and know it by touch, of which we are capable." So, they sought it out, and when they found it they groped about it. The first person, whose hand landed on the trunk, said, "This being is like a thick snake." For another one whose hand reached its ear, it seemed like a kind of fan. As for another person, whose hand was upon its leg, said, the elephant is a pillar like a tree-trunk. The blind man who placed his hand upon its side said the elephant, "is a wall." Another who felt its tail, described it as a rope. The last felt its tusk, stating the elephant is that which is hard, smooth and like a spear.

The degree of diversity in the IPE elephant is amply demonstrated in the formal literature. In preparation for this book, I undertook a systematic review of a representative sample of some three dozen textbooks or edited volumes of instructional materials intended for use in IPE courses in the United States (US), the United Kingdom (UK), or elsewhere in the English-speaking world – the area known to many as the Anglosphere. (The full list can be found in Appendix B.) Most of the sources offer some kind of formal definition of the field, but the variance among them, I found, was considerable. Different parts of the elephant are visualized. Some focus concretely on the traditional institutional dichotomy between markets and states. Others, more abstractly, think in terms of the broad behavioral categories of economics (implying more than just markets) and authority (implying more than just states). And yet others downplay institutions altogether, directing attention instead to generic social themes like conflict, power, or equity. The following are illustrative of the contrasts:

> Studying IPE is to understand the domestic and foreign economic policies of states and the ways these policies aggregate into a system of states. (Lairson and Skidmore 2017: 49)
> The relationship between state governments and the market economy is central to the study of IPE. (Smith et al. 2017: 3)
> IPE is the study of the interplay of economics and politics in the world arena. (Frieden et al. 2017: 1)
> [IPE is defined as] the complex relationship between power and wealth (or more specifically, between the political and economic domains) in international politics ... the link between political authority, on the one hand, and the system of production and distribution of wealth referred to as the market economy, on the other. (Stubbs and Underhill 2006: 3)
> IPE is concerned with international politics and international economics, that is to say, politics and economics beyond state borders. IPE focuses on the power relations between the world of states and that of economic actors on the international scene. (Paquin 2016: 5)
> Global Political Economy is a field of enquiry, a subject matter whose central focus is the interrelationship between public and private power in the allocation of scarce resources. (Ravenhill 2017: 20)
> IPE studies the political battle between winners and losers of global economic exchange. (Oatley 2018: 2)

Visions this dissimilar are not surprising, of course. Textbooks must necessarily be selective if they are to be anything less than encyclopedic. As one recent commentary pointed out: "Textbook narration is a boundary practice that ... establishes conditions of admissibility ... The selectivity in play reinforces boundary work delimiting the edges of the field" (Clift et al. 2021). Conceptions of the field, therefore, are bound to be to some extent personal and subjective. And of course there are also commercial considerations to take into account. Textbooks are published to earn a profit. Product differentiation is essential if any one volume is to stand out in a crowded field. Ultimately, sales are at stake.

But even if not surprising, diversity of such a degree tells us much about the state of IPE today. In a nutshell, the field is highly fragmented. Over time, scholarly debates have produced a goodly number of factions and disparate schools of thought – what one recent study calls the "networks and niches" of IPE (Seabrooke and Young 2017). Continues the same source: "IPE has no clearly established set of methods or behavioral assumptions that are recognized as 'best practice' across the globe" (Seabrooke and Young 2017: 288). Instead, as we shall see in Chapter 2, we have a wide range of competing and quite distinct research traditions, variously called paradigms, perspectives, or theoretical approaches. There is no sense of a prevailing order in the IPE universe – no uniform analytical core. Instead, as the dissimilarity of textbook definitions suggests, we have a big and colorful pot-pourri of styles, all contending for a share of attention. A key question for the future of IPE is what, if anything, can or should be done about all this diversity. I will return to that question in later chapters.

HISTORY

As a field of study, IPE is both very old and very young. It is old because the connections between economics and politics in international affairs have long been recognized and explored by keen observers. But it is also young because, until recently, it had not yet achieved the status of a formal, established academic discipline. The *modern* field of IPE, as we know it today, has actually been in existence for little more than half a century. Some speak of the emergence of a new field of study; for others, it is more the re-emergence of a much older scholarly tradition. Both views are, in a sense, correct.

A formal field of study may be said to exist when a coherent body of knowledge is developed to define a subject of inquiry. Recognized norms come to be employed to train and certify specialists; full-time employment opportunities become available in university teaching and research organizations; professional associations and learned societies are established to promote study and dialogue; and dedicated publishing venues open up to help disseminate new ideas and analysis. In short, an institutionalized network of scholars comes into being, a distinct research community with its own boundaries, rewards, and careers – an "invisible college," as it is sometimes called. In modern IPE, the invisible college did not begin to coalesce until near the end of the 1960s.

But there were precursors as well. In terms of intellectual antecedents, today's field actually has a long and distinguished heritage, going back to the liberal Enlightenment that spread across Europe in the seventeenth and eighteenth centuries. Even before there were separate disciplines of economics and political science, there was classical political economy – the label given to the study of economic aspects of public policy. Classical political economy encompassed three broad discourses: a practical discourse about policy, a normative discourse about the ideal relationship between the state and the economy, and a scientific discourse about the way the economy operates as a social system (Gamble 1995). All three discourses were key inspirations for today's invisible college. A recent commentary is right in insisting that "IPE did not undergo a pure virgin birth ... without classical political economy there could be no modern IPE" (Hobson 2013: 1031).

Classical political economy flourished throughout the eighteenth and early nineteenth centuries. From the French physiocrats and Adam Smith onward, the classical political economists all understood their subject to be a unified social science closely linked to the study of moral philosophy (Glaze 2015). Their perspective was self-consciously broad and inclusive. "The classical political economists were polymaths, who wrote on a variety of subjects," one expert has written (Watson 2005: 18). "They did not study 'the economy' as an enclosed and self-contained entity." The earliest university departments teaching the subject were all designated departments of political economy. John Stuart Mill's monumental summary of all Western economic knowledge in the mid-nineteenth century was pointedly entitled *Principles of Political Economy*.

Not long after Mill, however, a split opened up, fragmenting the social sciences in many parts of the world. Like an amoeba, classical political economy started to subdivide. In place of the earlier conception of a unified economic and political order, two separate realms were envisioned, representing two distinct spheres of human activity. One was "society," the private sector, based on contracts and decentralized market activity and concerned largely with issues of production and distribution. The other was the "state," the public sector, based on coercive authority and concerned with power, collective decision making, and the resolution of conflict. University departments were systematically reorganized to address the divergent agendas of the two realms. By the start of the twentieth century, the divorce of political science from economics was well under way, with fewer and fewer points of contact or communication remaining between them. As one source puts it, "Both disciplines became increasingly introspective" (Lake 2006: 758). It is significant that when the respected British economist Alfred Marshall decided to write a successor to Mill's *Principles* some half-century later, he purposely chose to call it *Principles of Economics*.

Not everyone elected to choose sides. In many places, particularly in Continental Europe and Latin America, the tradition of classical political economy lingered on, as recent research has highlighted (Helleiner 2020). The worldwide split between the two disciplines was deepest in the United States and Britain, where only a few hardy souls continued to resist the subdivision of the amoeba. Most of those were to be found at the radical fringes of US and British academia, heterodox observers outside the "respectable" mainstream of scholarship. These of course included Marxist or neo-Marxist circles on the Left, where the superstructure of politics was unquestioningly assumed to rest on a foundation defined by prevailing modes of production. They also included laissez-faire liberals or libertarians on the Right determined to preserve capitalism against the oppressive power of the state. For them, the proper goal was to uphold the "invisible hand" of market competition, not the "dead hand" of government.

There were also some notable exceptions closer to the orthodox mainstream in the Anglosphere. These were theorists whose contributions, to borrow a phrase from the Canadian scholar Randall Germain (2021), could be described as "IPE-inflected." Among them was the great British economist John Maynard Keynes, who cared deeply about the relationship between markets and the state. Another was Keynes's Cambridge colleague Joan Robinson, an under-appreciated scholar of more leftist persuasion. A third was Joseph Schumpeter, an Austrian polymath who taught for many years at Harvard and was best known for his magisterial treatise on *Capitalism, Socialism and Democracy* (Schumpeter 1942). A fourth was Albert Hirschman, author of many highly influential works, including *National Power and the Structure of Foreign Trade* (1945/1980) and *Exit, Voice, and Loyalty* (1970). Others included Karl Polanyi, E.H. Carr, and David Mitrany, a diverse trio whose writings, as Germain (2021) has shown, clearly prefigured important themes in modern IPE scholarship. Their efforts, Germain suggests, can be described as "nearly modern IPE."

For the most part, however, the void only grew deeper with time, especially among students of world affairs. References to political economy at the international level largely disappeared from polite conversation. By mid-twentieth century, in most places, the scholarly frontier dividing the economics and politics of global affairs had become firm and seemingly impassable – a Great Wall of silence. Mainstream researchers on either side of the wall rarely spoke to each other or even deigned to read one another's work. It was like a dialogue of the deaf.

The dichotomy was summarized acutely in a seminal article published in 1970 by the pioneering British scholar Susan Strange, provocatively entitled "International Economics and International Relations: A Case of Mutual Neglect" (Strange 1970). The void between international economics and international relations (IR) had endured for too long, Strange declared. Scholars from both traditions were neglecting fundamental changes in the world. The dialogue of the deaf should not be allowed to persist. A more modern approach to the study of international economic relations was needed – in her words, a determined effort at "bridge-building" to spotlight the crucial "middle ground" between economic and political analyses of international affairs. Here, for the first time, was a full and compelling case laid out for a new field of study, a clarion call expressed in the fierce and uncompromising manner that came to be Strange's trademark. The article was, for all intents and purposes, a manifesto.

Strange's summons to battle was by no means the sole spark to ignite a renewed interest in the political economy of international relations. By 1970, there were also other pioneers – principally but not exclusively in Britain and the US – who were beginning to grope their way toward reconnecting the two realms of inquiry, "reintegrating what had been somewhat arbitrarily split up" (Underhill 2000: 808). Change was in the air.

In the US, Richard Cooper published *The Economics of Interdependence* (Cooper 1968), highlighting the political challenges posed by the postwar era's accelerating interdependence of national economies, followed a few years later by Charles Kindleberger's justly celebrated *The World in Depression* (Kindleberger 1973), which introduced the notion of hegemonic stability. Raymond Vernon contributed *Sovereignty at Bay* (Vernon 1971), the first serious study of the multinational corporation, while Robert Keohane and Joseph Nye introduced us to the notion of transnationalism in their edited volume on *Transnational Relations and World Politics* (Keohane and Nye 1972), and Gilpin explored the role of power in the global economy (Gilpin 1975). On the British side of the pond the new trend was best represented by Strange's *Sterling and British Policy*, stressing the politics of international currency use (Strange 1971). In Latin America new perspectives on the global economy, emphasizing structural impediments to economic development, were being promoted by the Argentinian Raul Prebisch and the Brazilian Fernando Henrique Cardoso (Cohen 2019: chapter 7). And soon to come, as we shall see in the next chapter, were giants like the sociologist Immanuel Wallerstein, father of what came to be known as world-systems theory, and the Canadian Robert Cox, who proved to be a lasting inspiration for many younger scholars, particularly in Britain and Canada. Yet looking back, we can now appreciate how significant Strange's manifesto was. Its publication marked something of a tipping point. Never before had the brewing discontent among scholars been so effectively distilled and bottled. Nowhere else had the issue been posed in such concise and focused terms. As such, it is as good a candidate as any to mark the moment of birth (or rebirth) of the modern field of IPE.

LEARNING

Since Strange's call to battle, the newly born (or reborn) field has grown by leaps and bounds, attracting more and more devotees from a mélange of related disciplines. In the US the field has come to be dominated by political scientists and sociologists, with only a few economists inspired to consider the politics of the world economy seriously. To this day IPE remains a peripheral interest in most US economics departments. "To them," comments one informed observer ruefully, "IPE barely exists" (Aggarwal 2010: 894). Elsewhere the field has roots *inter alia* in international studies, international economics, comparative politics, sociology, and even international law and economic history. No wonder, then, that so many "networks and niches" have proliferated in IPE's invisible college. Extensive debates have raged on a wide range of issues.

So after all these debates, what have we learned? What do we know now that we did not know half a century ago?

Much depends on what we mean by learn. If the achievements of study are to be measured by our ability to make definitive statements about the world around us – to establish firm "social facts" – the level of learning may be rated as negligible at best. Specialists cannot point to a single non-trivial, non-obvious proposition on which there is universal agreement. The search for eternal truths has proved largely fruitless. Even after decades of effort, discord persists over the most basic issues of process and structure. Many theories have emerged, all intended to help deepen our understanding of how the world works. But none is accepted by all. An old jibe about the economics profession has it that if you laid all the economists in the world end to end, you still would not reach agreement. The same, regrettably, may be said of IPE. As Stephen Krasner, another of modern IPE's pioneers, ruefully acknowledged in a later reflection on the field, explanations "have, in some specific cases, been deeply illuminating, but no one has presented a coherent general theory" (Krasner 1996: 110).

But is that the best way to measure learning? Perhaps Gertrude Stein got it right. On her deathbed, surrounded by her closest confidants, the legendary literary figure is reputed to have asked: "What is the answer?" When no one dared to respond, it is said, she then added: "In that case, what is the question?" The point is apt. We may not know the answers, but at least we can learn how to ask the right questions – how to address the substantive content of our inquiry. For many, that is the true test of an academic field like IPE. "I use the term 'political economy,'" Gilpin once wrote, "simply to indicate a set of questions to be examined" (Gilpin 1987: 9). A more recent source concurs that IPE is best understood as a "question-asking field" (Watson 2005: 15). "The genius of [IPE]," adds a third, "lies in problem posing, rather than problem solving" (Dickins 2006: 480). Students of the subject may never agree on how the world works. But at least it should be possible to agree on how to *study* how the world works.

To facilitate that study, IPE has gradually developed a substantial number of critical concepts and analytical tools. Collectively, these may be regarded as the field's greatest contribution to learning. Among them was the early notion of hegemonic stability: Kindleberger's controversial idea that global economic health was somehow dependent on the presence of a single dominant power. Later came assorted concepts like international regimes and institutions, transnationalism and complex interdependence, regionalism and globalization, relational and structural power, network effects and inter-state diffusion, and much more – all generated to improve our vocabulary and help frame inquiry. Compared to where we were when the modern field first (re-)emerged in the 1960s and 1970s, we are now much better equipped to explore the ins and outs of the global economy. Our toolkit is far richer.

In effect, that takes us back to the definition of the field with which we started – Gilpin's "reciprocal and dynamic interaction in international relations of the pursuit of wealth and the pursuit of power." Few students of IPE would disagree with the idea that our subject, in broadest terms, is about the mutually endogenous and ever-changing nexus of interactions between economics and politics beyond the confines of a single state, an amalgam of market studies and political analysis. These are the core elements of the world that we want to study – the common denominator of the field.

The devil, of course, is in the details. At the broadest level, we may all accept the same common denominator. But try to get any more specific and differences quickly emerge. Two decades after Strange issued her "Mutual Neglect" manifesto, two of her followers were lamenting that "scholars still debate what exactly should be included in the set of questions that defines IPE" (Murphy and Tooze 1991: 2). And three decades further on, debates over agenda continue to roil the field (Best et al. 2021; LeBaron et al. 2021). As interest in the subject has continued to spread, differences, it seems, have grown ever deeper. Across the invisible college as a whole, individuals and factions emphasize entirely distinct sets of issues. Laments one younger scholar: "What was supposed to represent a bridge between 'international politics' and 'international economics' is now an ever more fragmented field" (Antunes de Oliveira 2020). I will return to this matter in Chapter 5.

ACHIEVEMENTS

Despite its failure to establish eternal truths, IPE must be regarded as a phenomenal success story. The field can boast of a number of key achievements. I will highlight four strengths in particular.

To begin with, IPE *exists*. That, in itself, is no small accomplishment. From its modest beginnings half a century ago, the newly (re)born field has come to be firmly ensconced in the academic firmament. Students flock to take IPE courses, attracted by its interdisciplinarity and attentiveness to pressing global issues. Colleges and universities now regularly hire specialists in IPE, and in many cases have developed distinct degree programs in the subject. Literally dozens of textbooks, readers, surveys, and handbooks are available for instructional purposes. New journals devoted specifically to research in the field have taken root, including the likes of the *Review of International Political Economy* (*RIPE*) and *New Political Economy* (*NPE*), both founded in the 1990s. Likewise, an impressive range of publishers have made IPE one of their specialties, including both prestigious university presses like Cambridge, Chicago, Cornell, Oxford, and Princeton and highly respected commercial houses such as Edward Elgar, Lynne Rienner, Palgrave Macmillan, Polity, and Routledge.

Perhaps most important of all, a small crowd of professional bodies has sprung up around the world to promote networking and debate. In the US, scholars have both the IPE Section of the International Studies Association (ISA) and the IPE Society (IPES) to choose from. Britain has the International Political Economy Group (IPEG), an organized section of the British International Studies Association (BISA) originally started by Susan Strange. Continental Europeans can choose between the Political Economy section of the long-established European Consortium for Political Research and the Consortium's newer offshoot, the European International Studies Association, and the Critical Political Economy Research Network of the European Sociological Association. Australians and Canadians each have their own International Political Economy Network. Latin America has the Latin American Political Economy Network. Turkey has the Turkish Political Economy Society. And even China, since 2010, has an International Political Economy Forum, which meets annually to discuss the country's latest IPE research. Our field's invisible college now spans the globe.

Moreover, not only does IPE exist – the field has securely established its right to exist. It has gained *legitimacy*. No longer is there an insurmountable Great Wall of silence dividing the separate specialties of international economics and IR. In the words of one recent commentary: "Whether international and transnational economic relations occupy an important place in political science research is no longer a question in today's world" (Wullweber 2019: 301). Admittedly, the wall has not been breached completely. Overall, the number of economists drawn to IPE remains relatively small; the majority of economists still prefer to hang out in the dismal science's separate lane. But for a critical mass of scholars from political science as well as from sociology and other cognate disciplines, the dialogue of the deaf has by now been replaced by a mutual recognition of the reciprocal connections that exist between the pursuit of wealth and the pursuit of power in global affairs. IPE's gift to the social sciences is the assurance that those connections will no longer be largely ignored or denied. References to political economy at the international level can now once again be included in polite conversation, as they were in the days of classical political economy.

Third, in substantive terms, it is evident that the field has been *enlightening*. IPE may not have succeeded in unearthing eternal truths. Indeed, we don't even agree much of the time on what are the right questions. But over the years we have learned a lot about practical matters in the world economy. These range *inter alia* from IPE's core issues of trade and finance to more specialized topics such as economic development, foreign investment, and the multinationalization of production. In more conceptual terms we have gained insight into the roles played by diverse actors in international economic affairs, from interest groups and social institutions at the local level to national governments and transnational forces at the global level. And we certainly now know more than we once did about the challenges involved in system governance and the operation of the world economy as a whole. We need only to consult any of today's many IPE textbooks to see how much progress has been made since the first tentative steps by the modern field's pioneers half a century ago.

Lastly, there is IPE's *diversity*, which arguably enhances the richness of the field. The development of factions or schools within any scholarly specialty is hardly an unfamiliar phenomenon in academic life, as the philosopher of science Thomas Kuhn (1962) long ago pointed out. Research communities commonly subdivide as experts seek out the comfort of others who share the same core values and assumptions. In the words of political psychologist Margaret Hermann (1998: 606), "Our identities become intertwined with the perspectives and points of view of the theoretical cohort to which we perceive ourselves belonging. And we tend to distance ourselves from those we do not understand or whose ideas seem discordant with our group's theoretical outlook." Differences then tend to be reinforced over time by divergent patterns of professional socialization, producing what the sociology of science calls distinct "discourse coalitions" (Wæver 1998). Niche proliferation – the emergence of multiple discourse coalitions within IPE's invisible college – is an altogether natural process.

A case can be made that intellectual clustering of this sort is by no means a bad thing. Scholars of international relations have long debated the relative merits of "singularism" (Grieco 2019) or "monism" (Wullweber 2019) versus theoretical pluralism. At issue is a fundamental question of research strategy. Should experts all subscribe to a single analytical perspective (singularism, monism) in hopes of maximizing mutual comprehension? Or would they be better off borrowing pragmatically from a variety of approaches to permit flexible adaptation to specific circumstances? By now, the risks of reducing a field of study to one uniform framework have come to be well understood. Without diverse approaches to choose from, key variables and relationships may be omitted from analysis, leading to under-specified theoretical models. Our understanding of the world may be left incomplete. Creativity may be stifled. A tolerance of diversity, by contrast, allows a hundred flowers to bloom (as Mao Zedong said in a rather different context).

As has often been noted, a research specialty without competing traditions can be compared to a monoculture in farming, dominated by a single biological species. Agricultural monocultures, we know, can be highly efficient since there is less unpredictability in cultivation and no need for trial and error. Similarly, in an academic monoculture, no time need be wasted arguing about basic standards or methodologies. But as Kathleen McNamara, a senior scholar of IPE, has rightly reminded us, "monocultures, be they intellectual or agricultural, are never healthy ... Intellectual monocultures, where one theoretical perspective, ontological position, and method are used exclusively, may well result in a ... dessication of the field of study" (McNamara 2011: 65, 70). Scholarship becomes arid and offers diminishing returns – a "quick ticket to extinction," as another senior scholar puts it (Denmark 2010: 899). A budding of multiple paradigms, by contrast, like the cultivation of mixed crops, can help to preserve a field's fertility. In this respect IPE can be thought of as a robust ecology, "a place with many flowers blooming" in the words of Seabrooke and Young (2017: 324). Innumerable species flourish, each offering its own take on the world. Opportunities for cross-pollination are abundant. That surely must be regarded as a strength.

JOINT PROBLEMS

Despite the success of IPE's story, however, deepening shadows loom. Acute pathologies have accumulated over time which threaten to erode the reputation and influence of the field. I will begin here with IPE's *joint* problems, highlighting four challenges in particular.

First is the *downside of diversity*. It may well be that in farming, a mixture of crops can make a field fecund. But in the academic world, a multiplication of species can also result in little more than dissonance and discord: a wild mass of weeds. Half a century of modern IPE scholarship has not in any way cumulated into a holistic body of knowledge. That makes any sort of generalization difficult. For many specialists, the lack of a uniform analytical core is a cause of considerable discomfort, as I have learned from private correspondence. *Sub rosa*, worries about fragmentation abound. "IPE has become a discipline of tribes," laments one colleague, "each clinging to its own chosen and preferred mental universe." Another complains that the field lacks a distinct "center of gravity." And yet others use words like balkanization, cacophony, or even chaos. Diversity on such a broad scale may signal ill-health, not strength. Disarray like this, jibes one long-time member of the invisible college, "is an excellent sign that a research program has become unproductive" (Denmark 2010: 898).

Much depends on the degree of communication between factions. Arguably, the problem is not diversity as such but rather how well diverse discourse coalitions manage to cohabit. Are they open to alternative points of view? Are they willing to learn from one another? Are they even aware of the existence of competing schools of thought? The kind of socialization within separate cohorts that Hermann (1998) talks about can build up a powerful momentum of its own. Factions may begin to distance themselves so much that they become effectively insular, if not isolated, foregoing the benefits of cross-fertilization. Knowledge comes to be segregated into separate silos, and new dialogues of the deaf emerge. That is what happened to the classical political economy of the Enlightenment when economists and political scientists eventually stopped talking to each other. It can in fact happen to any academic specialty – including today's IPE.

Indeed, our field today would seem to be at particular risk, judging from the way the subject is typically taught around the world. Too often, in assigned readings and class lectures, students are exposed at most to a broad contrast of orthodoxy versus heterodoxy in what Seabrooke and Young (2017) call a "reduction to polarity." Worse, in many graduate programs, where future generations of scholars are trained, instruction offers little more than a single version of IPE – something approaching a monoculture in miniature. It was not always that way. As recently as the 1990s, as McNamara (2011) points out, graduate courses at top research universities typically ranged across a diverse group of authors. In her words, "theoretical and methodological pluralism reined" (sic) (McNamara 2011: 66). But in more recent decades the coverage of most programs has grown increasingly sparse, with – as McNamara puts it – "big chunks of scholarship ... completely left off" (McNamara 2011: 67). The trend is unfortunate. Aspiring researchers may believe that they are joining a broad invisible college. In fact, without even knowing it, many instead are being initiated into a narrower faction, conditioned to remain loyal to one tradition among many. Consciously or unconsciously, they become members of a single discourse coalition, and insularity is reinforced. In the words of Peter Katzenstein, one more pioneer of modern IPE:

> The elimination of pluralistic approaches to the subject of IPE in the seminars taught in the leading graduate programs is a more serious matter that bodes ill for the IPE field. When important intellectual issues touching on ontology, epistemology and theory are no longer taught, the next generation of scholar

[sic] will no longer be aware of the choices and trade-offs we all confront in our research. And that makes reorientation and fresh starts more difficult in any field of scholarship. (Katzenstein 2011: 110)

Why worry?, some might ask. At least students are acquiring some grasp of the field, even if not the whole picture. But that way lies misconception and a potentially distorted perception of reality. As an old Yiddish saying puts it, a half-truth is a whole lie. Students deserve the whole truth. To get it, they must be reminded that there are in fact multiple versions of IPE, each with its own distinct personality. Otherwise, the fragmentation of the field can only be expected to grow worse. In the words of Anna Leander, a prominent European scholar: "The coexistence of a multiplicity of scientific approaches is unlikely to leave any trace unless scholars are forced to talk to each other" (Leander 2009: 325).

A second broad failing is a *lack of policy engagement*. In principle, the nature of IPE, with its broad multidisciplinary foundation combining both of the narrower specialties of economics and IR, should be expected to give members of the invisible college an advantage in formulating sound advice on global economic issues. Yet in practice we see remarkably little contribution to policy discourse. Only a relatively small minority in the field seem moved to enter directly into the public forum. As one colleague has suggested to me, "our discipline does not do too well with regard to societal impact." At least in part, this deficiency seems to be due to the nature of the incentive structures that typify university life. Tenure, promotion, and other marks of achievement in the academic world are awarded mostly on the basis of formal research rather than policy-related contributions. Hence most IPE specialists, like their counterparts in other social science disciplines, tend to write primarily for their fellow scholars rather than for a broader public audience. Their aim is to meet the highly refined demands of the academic peer-review process. The result is a literature that is largely unintelligible to readers outside the boundaries of the field and contributes little, if anything, to applied policy debate. I will have more to say on this matter in Chapter 3.

Third is a failing that might best be described as *narrowness*. It is true that the field has succeeded in promoting enlightenment on many aspects of the world economy. But it is equally true that to this day, much that might seem to be of potential importance remains largely unexplored – issues that arguably could deserve more attention than they have typically received to date. These include, in particular, a wide variety of social topics such as race, gender, class, and culture. IPE researchers are not unaware that there may be many gaps in the field's coverage and certainly are not reluctant to talk about them. Self-criticism erupts frequently. Illustrative was a two-day workshop in March 2019 at the Sheffield Political Economy Research Institute (SPERI) in England. Entitled "Political Economy on Trial," the workshop brought together leading scholars from Europe and North America to discuss "blind spots" in IPE. Many of the papers were subsequently published in a double special issue of the journals *NPE* and *RIPE* (Best et al. 2021; LeBaron et al. 2021). But is the criticism warranted? Must IPE address every issue under the sun? What are the limits? It is not easy to know where to draw the line between the essential and the non-essential for purposes of research. I will address that challenge in Chapter 5.

A final failing is *timidity* – a disinclination by many in the field to address really big and important questions of global change. More often than not, researchers tend to restrict themselves to topics that are relatively limited in ambition and mostly quite narrow in scope – micro or mid-range issues that are more easily studied and have longer disciplinary histories to draw on. No one can deny that there are major changes going on in today's world economy. The distribution of power between states, as well as between states and market forces, is shifting dramatically. Nationalism, populism, and mercantilism are on the rise. High finance increasingly dominates commercial activity. New transnational forces are emerging, ranging from multinational corporations to organized criminal networks. (Some would say that there is not much difference between the two.) Existential challenges are posed by, *inter alia*, climate change, migration, contagious viruses, and water shortages. And technology is altering the very nature of work and the way we communicate with one another. Yet, strikingly, only a minority of scholars seems inclined to take on any of these mega-challenges seriously. The majority avert their eyes.

That was not the way modern IPE started. Back in the 1960s and 1970s, the pioneers of the newly (re)born field did not hesitate to address the big and important global questions of their own day. They were ambitious and thrived on what Keohane has described as "joyous contestation" (Keohane 2011: 37). In his words, "We were young, exuberant, and friends with one another, neither expecting nor wanting general agreement ... To us, the under-explored area of political economy offered irresistible territory for intellectual adventure and, one might say, conquest" (Keohane 2011: 37). Today, the thrill of intellectual adventure seems little in evidence. Even in more radical circles, most scholars seem loathe to stray very far from the familiar.

That too is a source of discomfort for many in the field. Says one senior figure, in private correspondence, "I worry that we have stopped asking bigger, broader questions and instead focus almost entirely on narrower issues." A good number of colleagues, junior as well as senior, admit to me in confidence that they find much of the IPE literature today to be arid, unexciting, even a little depressing. In the words of one, "IPE [is] stuck in a bit of a rut." Another says that it fails "to enrich the intellectual imagination." A third uses the word "tired." My own word for it is "boring" (Cohen 2010).

DIVISIVE PROBLEMS

In addition to its troublesome joint problems, IPE also suffers from a number of critical *divisive* problems – matters that sharply divide different groups of specialists within the field of study. Combat between cohorts can be intense. At times it appears as if the field has gone to war with itself. Four divisive problems stand out.

Most prominent are conflicts over *paradigms*. Each of IPE's many "networks and niches" has its own theoretical perspective – its own set of basic ideas and assumptions about how the world works. The need for a paradigm in scholarly discourse is obvious. Analytical tractability demands it. As one senior scholar summarizes, "We cannot make progress without paradigms to guide research" (Lake 2011: 51). Reality is far too complex to be captured in its entirety by any single model. Instead, we are all compelled to simplify reality in one way or another in order to render it explicable. In short, we make assumptions. In the words of a trio of IPE theorists: "IPE, and social sciences in general, would not be possible without foundational assumptions [choosing] to privilege certain ways of viewing the world over others" (van Apeldoorn et al. 2011: 216). Years ago, economist Robert Heilbroner defined paradigms as "systems of thought and belief by which [actors] explain ... how their social system operates and what principles it exemplifies" (Heilbroner 1985: 107). Synonyms include words like perspective, model, theory, or ideology. Paradigms can be thought of as total belief systems. Ultimately, they are an act of faith, not unlike religion.

Not surprisingly, therefore, competition between paradigms can become remarkably rancorous, almost like religious war in tone. Belief systems form the basis for the emergence of discourse coalitions. Once factions of the invisible college come to be consolidated, their intellectual commitments tend to be grasped tenaciously, often stubbornly resistant to logic or contrary evidence. Where some researchers see rational behavior, others see ideas or coercion at work. Where some see natural harmony, others see nothing but conflict. Where some see politics driving economics, others see the dominance of select social actors or the global capitalist system. In IPE today diverse schools of thought accuse each other of all sorts of sins, contributing to the sense of cacophony that pervades the field. In the place of a dialogue of the deaf, we have mutual distrust, even disgust. Charges of heresy abound.

Is there any way to reduce the level of rancor? Can contrasting perspectives somehow be reconciled? Or is the field condemned forever to fatal fragmentation? I will have more to say about these questions in later chapters.

A second problem involves *methodology*. Few in the field would question the importance of empirical evidence as a foundation for sound research. As one colleague has insisted to me, "IPE's strength lies in its empiricism." But bare facts alone are not enough. The key question is: What analytical techniques will suffice for the purpose of interpreting those facts and giving them meaning? For many IPE specialists, a commitment to formal quantitative or qualitative methods is an absolute imperative – the more demanding, the better. But for many others, this is all a "methods fetish" – an obsession with technique at the expense of substantive knowledge. Too often, research is channeled toward narrow questions that happen to be the most amenable to rigorous testing. As another colleague complains, scholarship is too often judged solely on the basis of "methodological litmus tests [which] seem to divide us more than assist us." On this issue the field is very far from consensus.

A third problem involves *time* – specifically, the question of whether our studies should be looking more to past times or to the future. In practice, much IPE research tends to be ahistorical. The British scholar John M. Hobson calls this a "presentist pathology" (Hobson 2021: 5). Where history does play a role, analysis tends to be mostly backward-looking on the not unreasonable grounds that better understanding of what happened yesterday might offer useful insight into what could happen in similar circumstances tomorrow. As Mark Twain is alleged to have said, history doesn't repeat itself but it often rhymes. Concentration on the past, however, can result in a failure to anticipate adequately all the risks of the future. Historically oriented studies may teach us something about "known knowns" and even "known unknowns." But they could miss out completely in preparing us for "unknown unknowns" – the kind of incipient or emerging trends that have no close antecedent to guide us. The relevance of the past is subject to rapid obsolescence as historical circumstances evolve. Of course, no one honestly believes it is possible to forecast the future with any degree of accuracy. (In the words of the great philosopher Yogi Berra, prediction is difficult, particularly if it involves the future.) But a case can be made that IPE would be better served if research energies were applied more to exploring possible futures rather than to the resurrection and dissection of increasingly antiquated pasts.

Finally, there is a problem that we might label *materialism* – a question whether behavior in IPE is more about material factors or cognition. Many specialists, in their search for enduring causal relationships, are content to focus entirely on "real" variables in the world economy. That means elements that can be priced and measured, such as production, income, investment, and trade. But many others in the field insist instead on the importance of cognitive factors such as ideas, beliefs, norms, and intersubjective understandings, which are rather more difficult to pin down in quantitative terms. In principle, there is no reason why the two classes of explanatory variables cannot be integrated in a single analytical framework. It is surely not unreasonable to assume that they might interact naturally on a regular basis. In practice, however, despite increasing efforts to merge the two approaches, infighting over the issue persists and is often quite bruising.

QUESTIONS

Overall, then, it is evident that the field of IPE is troubled. Such a wide array of challenges, including both joint problems and divisive problems, cannot be regarded as a sign of robust good health. Quite the contrary, in fact. In many respects the field is ailing, a victim of its own neglect and drift. For too long pathologies have been allowed to breed uncontrollably, threatening the very viability of the field. There is much about IPE today that must be rethought.

To begin, we must first establish what we are thinking *about*. That is the purpose of Chapter 2, which sketches out the broad contours of the field of IPE as it exists around the world today. A Big Picture is provided in the form of a taxonomy of the field's principal analytical approaches. At the heart of IPE is the familiar dichotomy between *orthodox* and *heterodox* paradigms (alternatively, "mainstream" versus "radical" or "critical" perspectives). For most scholars in the field, that is the common starting point. Beyond that basic dichotomy, I then outline the most popular variations on each of the two themes. Theoretical approaches are differentiated from one another by five key defining characteristics: ontology, agenda, purpose, boundaries, and epistemology. The chapter serves to demonstrate the high degree of pluralism that has come to characterize modern IPE. A comprehensive look at the Big Picture should be of value not only to students but even to veteran specialists in the field who have spent too long working in a single theoretical tradition.

Taking Chapters 1 and 2 together, it would appear that most of the pathologies assailing IPE can be reduced to three core questions. These are:

1. What is the purpose of the field? Call this the *Why* question. Why do we study IPE?
2. What can be done or should be done about diversity in the field? Call this the *How* question. How should we study IPE?
3. What issues should be addressed in the field? Call this the *What* question. What is the proper agenda for IPE?

Each of these three questions is the subject of a subsequent chapter (Chapters 3–5). In each of the three chapters, broad prescriptions are suggested to help remedy the field. In a final chapter (Chapter 6), I offer a more detailed plan of action and take up the all-important practicalities of effective implementation.

Chapter 3 addresses purpose: the Why question. Reflecting on the field as it exists today, it is clear that for most specialists, preferred motives are largely "academic." Most emphasize positivist explanations and/or normative critiques rather than serious policy engagement outside the ivory tower. The chapter argues that the health of the field is threatened by two dangerous pathologies, which I label "mutual animus" and "unilateral disdain." Mutual animus pits orthodoxy against heterodoxy (mainstream versus radical or critical) and could lead to irreversible fragmentation of the field. Unilateral disdain discourages policy-oriented research and risks condemning the field to irrelevance. In both cases, the chapter concludes, prescriptions are possible but will take considerable effort to be put into effect.

Chapter 4 aims to think anew about the abundant diversity of the field of IPE: the How question. Diversity gives us a broad range of paradigms and research traditions to work with. Though pluralism can be a blessing, the chapter argues that today it is more often a curse, exposing the field to another pair of dangerous pathologies. These are "inadvertent omission" and "overt opposition." Inadvertent omission refers to the intellectual myopia that afflicts much of the field, limiting familiarity with the full range of available theoretical approaches. Overt opposition describes the possibility that other perspectives may be familiar but are actively rejected, threatening animus and perhaps even paradigm war. Effective remedies are not easy to find. The key prescription, the chapter contends, is not to ignore or deplore diversity but rather to make the best possible use of it. Most promising is a strategy known as "analytic eclecticism," which seeks to go "beyond paradigms" by looking for hidden commonalities and connections among competing theories and models. Gaining widespread adoption of analytic eclecticism, however, will be a challenge. Here too, considerable effort will be needed.

Chapter 5 takes up the matter of agenda: the What question. Among IPE scholars, the feeling is widespread that too many substantive issues have yet to receive the attention they deserve. The field, it is said, has many "blind spots." But is IPE really too narrow? Wish lists are easy to conceive. The challenge, the chapter argues, is to know where to draw the line. What is or is not in the field's comparative advantage? The limits to IPE's agenda are bound to be elastic; more importantly, they are also likely to vary across factions of the invisible college depending on how each discourse coalition answers the Why and How questions. What purpose is to be served by taking up any particular issue and what analytical approach is to be used to dissect it? Realistically, the diversity of the field must be expected to give rise to a variety of possible agendas. Much can be learned, therefore, if each school of thought pays more attention to what others are interested in. A review of some half-dozen alleged gaps in the field illustrates how much value can be added to research by keeping an open mind to alternative priorities.

Chapter 6, lastly, addresses the Big Challenge of implementation. In practical terms, how can we apply the prescriptions suggested in Chapters 3–5? Some degree of resistance to change must be expected. Remedies, therefore, need to come with a set of instructions – a realistic strategy to overcome stubborn forces of inertia. Like most academic specialties, IPE is replete with powerful gatekeepers with an almost unlimited capacity to set standards and define goals. These include instructors, personnel committees, funding sources, program chairs, and book and journal editors. To countervail their authority, the chapter concludes, leadership is needed from the field's many organized associations and societies which, collectively, have the capacity to exercise some degree of leverage over gatekeeping practices. A credible plan of action is possible including both sticks and carrots designed to revitalize our beleaguered field of study. The health of IPE can be restored.

REFERENCES

Aggarwal, Vinod K. (2010), "I Don't Get No Respect: The Travails of IPE," *International Studies Quarterly* 54:3, 893–5.

Antunes de Oliveira, Felipe (2020), "Of Economic Whips and Political Necessities: A Contribution to the International Political Economy of Uneven and Combined Development," *Cambridge Review of International Affairs*, DOI: 10.1080/09557571.2020.1818690.

Best, Jacqueline, Colin Hay, Genevieve LeBaron, and Daniel Mügge (2021), "Seeing and Not-seeing Like a Political Economist: The Historicity of Contemporary Political Economy and its Blind Spots," *New Political Economy* 28:2, 217–28.

Clift, Ben, Peter M. Kristensen, and Ben Rosamond (2021), "Remembering and Forgetting IPE: Disciplinary History as Boundary Work," *Review of International Political Economy* (forthcoming).

Cohen, Benjamin J. (2010), "Are IPE Journals Becoming Boring?," *International Studies Quarterly* 54:3, 887–91.

Cohen, Benjamin J. (2019), *Advanced Introduction to International Political Economy*, 2nd edition (Cheltenham, UK and Northampton, MA, USA: Edward Elgar Publishing).

Cooper, Richard N. (1968), *The Economics of Interdependence: Economic Policy in the Atlantic Community* (New York: McGraw Hill).

Denemark, Robert A. (2010), "Toward a Vibrant IPE Literature: Commiserating with Cohen," *International Studies Quarterly* 54:3, 897–9.

Dickins, Amanda (2006), "The Evolution of International Political Economy," *International Affairs* 82:3, 479–92.

Frieden, Jeffry A., David A. Lake, and J. Lawrence Broz (2017), "Introduction," in Jeffry A. Frieden, David A. Lake and J. Lawrence Broz, eds., *International Political Economy: Perspectives on Global Power and Wealth*, 6th edition (New York and London: Norton), 1–17.

Gamble, Andrew (1995), "The New Political Economy," *Political Studies* 43:3, 516–30.

Germain, Randall (2021), "Nearly Modern IPE? Insights from IPE at Mid-Century," *Review of International Studies* 47:4, 528-48.

Gilpin, Robert (1975), *U.S. Power and the Multinational Corporation* (New York: Basic Books).

Gilpin, Robert (1987), *The Political Economy of International Relations* (Princeton, NJ: Princeton University Press).

Glaze, Simon (2015), "Schools Out: Adam Smith and Pre-Disciplinary International Political Economy," *New Political Economy* 20:5, 679–701.

Grieco, Joseph M. (2019), "The Schools of Thought Problem in International Relations," *International Studies Review* 21:3, 424–46.

Heilbroner, Robert L. (1985), *The Nature and Logic of Capitalism* (New York: Norton).

Helleiner, Eric (2020), "Globalizing the Historical Roots of IPE," in Ernesto Vivares, ed., *The Routledge Handbook to Global Political Economy* (New York: Routledge), 43–57.

Hermann, Margaret (1998), "One Field, Many Perspectives: Building the Foundations for Dialogue," *International Studies Quarterly* 42:4, 605–24.

Hirschman, Albert O. (1945/1980), *National Power and the Structure of Foreign Trade* (Berkeley and Los Angeles: University of California Press).

Hirschman, Albert O. (1970), *Exit, Voice, and Loyalty: Responses to Decline in Firms, Organizations, and States* (Cambridge, MA: Harvard University Press).

Hobson, John M. (2013), "Part I – Revealing the Eurocentric Foundations of IPE: A Critical Historiography of the Discipline from the Classical to the Modern Era," *Review of International Political Economy* 20:5, 1024–54.

Hobson, John M. (2021), *Multicultural Origins of the Global Economy: Beyond the Western-Centric Frontier* (New York: Cambridge University Press).

Katzenstein, Peter J. (2011), "Mid-Atlantic: Sitting on the Knife's Sharp Edge," in Nicola Phillips and Catherine E. Weaver, eds., *International Political Economy: Debating the Past, Present and Future* (London: Routledge), 105–15.

Keohane, Robert O. (2011), "The Old IPE and the New," in Nicola Phillips and Catherine E. Weaver, eds., *International Political Economy: Debating the Past, Present and Future* (London: Routledge), 35–44.

Keohane, Robert O. and Joseph S. Nye, Jr., eds. (1972), *Transnational Relations and World Politics* (Cambridge, MA: Harvard University Press).

Kindleberger, Charles P. (1973), *The World in Depression 1929–1939* (Berkeley and Los Angeles: University of California Press).

Krasner, Stephen D. (1996), "The Accomplishments of International Political Economy," in Steve Smith, Ken Booth, and Marysia Zalewski, eds., *International Theory: Positivism and Beyond* (New York: Cambridge University Press), 108–27.

Kuhn, Thomas S. (1962), *The Structure of Scientific Revolutions* (Chicago: University of Chicago Press).

Lairson, Thomas D. and David Skidmore (2017), *The Struggle for Power and Wealth in a Globalizing World* (New York and London: Routledge).

Lake, David A. (2006), "International Political Economy: A Maturing Interdiscipline," in Barry R. Weingast and Donald A. Wittman, eds., *The Oxford Handbook of Political Economy* (New York: Oxford University Press), 757–77.

Lake, David A. (2011), "TRIPS across the Atlantic: Theory and Epistemology in IPE," in Nicola Phillips and Catherine E. Weaver, eds., *International Political Economy: Debating the Past, Present and Future* (London: Routledge), 45–52.

Leander, Anna (2009), "Why We Need Multiple Stories about the Global Political Economy," *Review of International Political Economy* 16:2, 321–8.

LeBaron, Genevieve, Daniel Mügge, Jacqueline Best, and Colin Hay (2021), "Blind Spots in IPE: Marginalized Perspectives and Neglected Trends in Contemporary Capitalism," *Review of International Political Economy* 28:2, 283–94.

McNamara, Kathleen (2011), "Of Intellectual Monocultures and the Study of IPE," in Nicola Phillips and Catherine E. Weaver, eds., *International Political Economy: Debating the Past, Present and Future* (London: Routledge), 64–73.

Murphy, Craig N. and Roger Tooze (1991), "Getting Beyond the 'Common Sense' of the IPE Orthodoxy," in Craig N. Murphy and Roger Tooze, eds., *The New International Political Economy* (Boulder, CO: Lynne Rienner), 1–31.

Oatley, Thomas H. (2018), *International Political Economy*, 6th edition (New York and London: Routledge).

Paquin, Stéphane (2016), *Theories of International Political Economy: An Introduction* (Toronto: Oxford University Press).

Ravenhill, John, ed. (2017), *Global Political Economy*, 5th edition (Oxford and New York: Oxford University Press).

Schumpeter, Joseph (1942), *Capitalism, Socialism and Democracy* (New York: Harper and Brothers).

Seabrooke, Leonard and Kevin L. Young (2017), "The Networks and Niches of International Political Economy," *Review of International Political Economy* 24:2, 288–331.

Smith, Roy, Imad El-Anis, and Christopher Farrands (2017), *International Political Economy in the 21st Century: Contemporary Issues and Analyses*, 2nd edition (London and New York: Routledge).

Strange, Susan (1970), "International Economics and International Relations: A Case of Mutual Neglect," *International Affairs* 46:2, 304–15.

Strange, Susan (1971), *Sterling and British Policy: A Political Study of an International Currency in Decline* (London: Oxford University Press).

Stubbs, Richard and Geoffrey R.D. Underhill (2006), "Introduction: Conceptualizing the Changing Global Order," in Richard Stubbs and Geoffrey R.D. Underhill, eds., *Political Economy and the Changing Global Order*, 3rd edition (Toronto, Oxford, and New York: Oxford University Press), 3–23.

Underhill, Geoffrey R.D. (2000), "State, Market, and Global Political Economy: Genealogy of an (Inter?) Discipline," *International Affairs* 76:4, 805–24.

van Apeldoorn, Bastiaan, Ian Bruff, and Magnus Ryner (2011), "The Richness and Diversity of Critical IPE Perspectives: Moving Beyond the Debate on the 'British School,'" in Nicola Phillips and Catherine Weaver, eds., *International Political Economy: Debating the Past, Present and Future* (London: Routledge), 215–22.

Vernon, Raymond (1971), *Sovereignty at Bay: The Multinational Spread of U.S. Enterprises* (New York: Basic Books).

Wæver, Ole (1998), "The Sociology of a Not So International Discipline: American and European Developments in International Relations," *International Organization* 52:4, 687–727.

Watson, Matthew (2005), *Foundations of International Political Economy* (New York: Palgrave Macmillan).

Wullweber, Joscha (2019), "Monism vs. Pluralism, the Global Financial Crisis, and the Methodological Struggle in the Field of International Political Economy," *Competition and Change* 23:3, 287–311.

2. The Big Picture

The aim of this chapter is to sketch out the broad contours of the field of International Political Economy (IPE) as it exists around the world today – what I call the Big Picture. Given how balkanized the field has become, that is no easy task. Many IPE specialists believe that without an agreed center of gravity, the field has simply become too diverse to be summarized in a single coherent portrait. The skepticism is understandable. But remember the ancient proverb about forests and trees. With even the most chaotic clump of trees, we are not necessarily condemned to losing sight of the forest. We just have to step back far enough to take it all in. For all of IPE's tribalism, a Big Picture is not impossible.

ATTRIBUTES

The parameters of the field of IPE can best be represented by a taxonomy or classification of the principal theoretical approaches that compete for the attention (and allegiance) of scholars and students. Taken together, IPE's diverse paradigms give us a good idea of where the outer edges of the field are located. But how do we distinguish among all of IPE's many perspectives? What attributes are most salient in differentiating one approach from another? I contend that for the purpose of painting a useful Big Picture, five dimensions stand out: ontology, agenda, purpose, boundaries, and epistemology. Together, these five defining characteristics provide us with a useful analytical guide for comparing and contrasting alternative conceptions of the field.

First is *ontology*, from the Greek for "things that exist." Ontology is about investigating reality: the nature, essential properties, and relations of being. What are the basic units of analysis in our research, and what are their key relationships? Do we primarily study individual persons? Firms? Classes? Social units? Sovereign states? Or the "system" as a whole? For many researchers, particularly in the United States (US), the proper focus is the state. Analysis is – or should be – strictly state-centric, which is why in America and often elsewhere our field of study is known as *International* Political Economy rather than *Global*

Political Economy (GPE). The adjective "international" signals that the focus is on nation states and the relations between them, rather than on more global structures or processes. In other research traditions, by contrast, it is the broad overall system that is or should be of more interest. Hence for many scholars the label should be GPE rather than IPE, to emphasize that distinction. In practice both designations are legitimate, though representing distinctly different ontologies.

Second is *agenda*. What are the most salient issues to be addressed? Are we primarily interested in matters relating to material welfare – the production and distribution of goods and services for final use – as emphasized by the discipline of economics? Alternatively, is our interest more in issues of politics and governance – decision making, cooperation, and the management of conflict – as stressed by political scientists? Or are both economic and political considerations merely a means to an entirely different end – an interest, perhaps, in social structures or class relations? Do we emphasize more the role of power in determining economic outcomes, or rather the part that economic scarcity plays in shaping political behavior? Should we focus on markets or hierarchies? Are our horizons primarily local or regional, or does our perspective extend to the intercontinental and global? And what are the links among these different geographic levels of analysis? In the real world, of course, everything is in a sense intertwined – "mutually endogenous," to adopt a phrase beloved of social scientists. Nonetheless, for analytical purposes it is necessary to establish priorities about what is to be considered more or less central.

Third is *purpose*. What is the goal of research? The choice here is tripartite. Is our aim "positive," intended primarily to enhance our objective understanding of how the world works? Is it, rather, more "normative," hoping to make the world a better place to live? Or is it consultative, aiming to offer practical policy advice to governments and other authoritative decision makers? Do we study IPE to gain more insight into underlying causal relationships, to promote the cause of social justice, or to address current policy challenges? Is our motivation comprehension, critique, or counsel?

Fourth are *boundaries*. Where do we draw a line around our multidisciplinary (or interdisciplinary) field of study? How receptive are we to ideas or insights from other specialties beyond IPE's roots in economics and political science? How important are contributions from closely related disciplines like sociology, history, geography, or psychology? What role is played by cultural, gender, or racial studies? And what about other more distant areas of scholarship such as anthropology, law, religion, or philosophy? Should the boundaries of our field be drawn tightly to provide a more parsimonious basis for theory-building? Or to quote Susan Strange, should inquiry be "unfenced ... open to all comers" (Strange 1984: ix)? The study of IPE, Strange argued, "would do well to stay an open range, like the old Wild West, accessible ... to literate people of all walks of life" (Strange 1991: 33).

Fifth, last but not least, is *epistemology*, from the Greek word for "knowledge." Epistemology has to do with the methods and grounds of knowing. What analytical techniques do we use to study the world? All theoretical inquiry, properly speaking, should begin with accurate observation of behavior and a close reading of available empirical evidence. But must our understanding be grounded primarily in rigorous quantitative or qualitative research methodologies? Or can we rely as well, or instead, on less formal approaches that rely to a greater extent on logical inference, intuition, or even pure speculation? IPE is a social science, but should the emphasis be on the social or the science?

CLASSIFICATIONS

The aim of this list of defining attributes is to provide criteria for a summary classification of our field's principal theoretical traditions. But we know that differences can exist along all these dimensions, combining in a variety of complex ways. Hence it is not always easy to know where to draw the lines between competing perspectives. Any set of labels to categorize paradigms is bound in some degree to be arbitrary – and therefore controversial. "Typologies are most useful," the noted scholar John Ravenhill has remarked, "when they have minimal within-type variance and maximum between-type variation" (Ravenhill 2008: 26). But classifications that achieve this ideal are hard to find. Alternative traditions may diverge along some dimensions even while converging on others; elements of several perspectives may overlap and intertwine, even in the minds of individual scholars. Like any healthy ecology, IPE's world is inherently messy. No wonder it has been called chaotic.

Indeed, the cacophony is such that some critics just throw up their hands, in effect overwhelmed by the notorious diversity of the field. Typical is the Norwegian Helge Hveem (2011), who questions whether we should even try to conceive of any sort of Big Picture. The field, he argues, is simply too much of a pot-pourri to be captured by any single system of classification. Though it is possible to sympathize with

Hveem's frustration, it does come across as something of a surrender of responsibility. We deserve more clarity than that.

Other scholars go to the opposite extreme, producing taxonomies of such density that they make the eyes glaze over. A representative example was offered recently by two prominent scholars, Leonard Seabrooke and Kevin Young (2017), who used highly refined community-detection methodologies to distinguish numerous "networks and niches" in IPE's thriving ecology – as many as a half-dozen or more distinct clusters of intellectual style at any given time. One can admire the erudition underlying such an analysis yet question its usefulness. The purpose of any typology should be to simplify and clarify, not overwhelm. The Seabrooke–Young analysis really does lose sight of the forest for the trees.

Between these extremes lie many possible systems of classification, each stressing one or some combination of our five defining attributes. Regrettably, there is no single optimum. There are many ways to organize our understanding of the field. Around the world, perhaps the most widely used classification system is based on an oft-noted dichotomy between what are described as either *orthodox* or *heterodox* theoretical perspectives. Orthodoxy (derived from ancient Greek for "right opinion") is often equated with the term "mainstream" though that by no means necessarily implies better or preferred. Heterodoxy (from the Greek for "deviation from orthodoxy"), conversely, aims to be more "radical" or "critical" in nature, challenging the mainstream to a greater or lesser extent. Orthodox approaches are more prevalent in the US, while heterogenous approaches are more widely found in the United Kingdom (UK) and elsewhere.

The distinction between orthodoxy and heterodoxy is familiar and widely used in the IPE literature. Even Seabrooke and Young, despite the many "networks and niches" in their analysis, admit that "Within IPE, the tension between American and non-American approaches has long been the focus" (Seabrooke and Young 2017: 291). Frequently, the dichotomy is highlighted simply by the choice of label between *Global* Political Economy and *International* Political Economy. Back in 2009 when Mark Blyth, a Scotsman teaching in the US, organized a collection of invited essays on the state of our field of study, he chose to follow earlier convention by using IPE in the title – not once but twice, in fact (Blyth 2009). A decade later, when a successor volume was put together by a prominent heterodox scholar from Latin America, IPE was replaced by GPE to signal a distinct shift of perspective (Vivares 2020). Throughout the collection the two acronyms IPE and GPE are used in the volume as synonyms for, respectively, orthodoxy and heterodoxy.

Orthodox approaches tend to be state-centric in their ontology and agenda, positivist in their purpose, narrow in their conception of the field's boundaries, and demanding in their choice of methodology. Heterodox approaches, conversely, are typically less state-centric, more normative, more inclined toward the open range advocated by Strange, and more relaxed about methods. Because of their emphasis on objectivity and rigor, orthodox scholars see themselves as more "serious" than their heterodox counterparts. Because of their emphasis on justice and inclusiveness, heterodox scholars see themselves as morally superior. Orthodox scholars are the puritans of IPE, earnest in their devotion to tradition. Heterodox scholars are more like free thinkers, determined to reject oppressive belief systems.

Following common practice, I too will make use here of the orthodox/heterodox divide as a first step in sketching out a Big Picture of the field. The advantage is that the dichotomy maximizes between-type variance. It is easy to know where to draw a line between contending paradigms. With this line the field can be defined simply in terms of two sharply contrasting styles.

Admittedly, there are disadvantages as well. Two issues, in particular, stand out. First, the blunt dichotomy between orthodoxy and heterodoxy obscures the role of researchers whose work more or less straddles the line between the two categories – scholars like Blyth, Jeffrey Chwieroth, Eric Helleiner, Jonathan Kirshner, Matthias Matthijs, Katherine McNamara, Louis Pauly, Jason Sharman, and Andrew Walter. Ravenhill calls these the "missing middle" – researchers whose work is important yet difficult to classify on the basis of the orthodox/heterodox divide alone. And, second, the dichotomy suppresses many crucial differences that can be found under each of the two broad headings. In reality, in each category there remains a considerable amount of within-type variance. For both reasons, therefore, further steps are needed to obtain a full appreciation of the range of perspectives to be found in IPE. The orthodox/heterodox divide must be treated as no more than a first approximation, helpful mainly as a starting point for more refined further discussion. Due attention must be paid as well to the many interesting variations that have been developed over the years within or across the two broad themes.

ORTHODOX PERSPECTIVES

Orthodox perspectives, as indicated, share a preference for a state-centric ontology, positivism, closed disciplinary boundaries, and rigorous methodology. Because approaches of this kind got an early start well over a half-century ago, they gradually came to acquire the mantle of scholarly orthodoxy. And because they are especially popular in the US, where there are more specialists in IPE than anywhere else in the world, orthodoxy in the field has come to be most closely identified with the conventional standards of mainstream US social science. Though its adherents can be found worldwide, many in the field today simply call it the American school (Cohen 2008).

The orthodox style, however, comes in many flavors, reflecting a multitude of intellectual traditions. Within the American school there are all sorts of debates over everything from the proper level of analysis to the salience of materialist versus cognitive motivations for behavior. Orthodoxy may be based on common premises, but it is by no means unanimous over how to build on that foundation (Cohen 2009). For many years, a once-popular American restaurant chain advertised itself as the home of 28 flavors of ice cream. The American school of IPE has even more.

The American School

From the start, American-style IPE has seen itself essentially as a sub-specialty of the study of international relations (IR) – in effect, a branch of political science. Foremost, this means that IPE in America is, above all, about sovereign states. As in the discipline of IR more generally, the state is seen as the fundamental locus of authority in world politics. No other actor enjoys the legitimacy that comes with internationally recognized sovereignty, nor can any other actor legally exercise the ultimate right of coercion. It is no surprise, therefore, that for the American style of IPE, ontology would be firmly state-centric. National governments are the core actors. State policymaking is the main concern. Other actors, whether domestic or transnational, are not ignored. But they enter the scene mainly insofar as they exercise some form of influence or constraint on government behavior.

Further, as indicated, most scholarship in the American style tends to hew closely to the methodological norms of conventional US social science. Priority is given to scientific method – what may be called a pure or hard science model. Analysis is based on the twin principles of positivism and empiricism, which hold that knowledge is best accumulated through an appeal to objective observation and the systematic evaluation of evidence using rigorous quantitative or qualitative techniques. Conjectures in some form are specified, based on deductive reasoning, and then tested for empirical accuracy – a process formally known as "hypothetico-deductivism." Grand comprehensive conceptualization on a global scale is generally eschewed. The style, instead, is essentially ahistorical. As often noted, systemic change does not generally enter the picture (Oatley 2021). Most emphasis is placed instead on micro- or mid-level theory, concentrating on narrow relationships isolated within a broader structure whose characteristics are unquestioned and assumed, implicitly, to be stable through time.

The purpose of analysis in the American school is to explain and understand how the world works, not to judge it. Normative concerns, for the most part, are downplayed. Serious scholarship is not to be sullied by personal values or policy advocacy. Theoretical inspiration is drawn largely from just two disciplines – modern IPE's twin ancestors of economics and political science. Ideas or insights from other scholarly specialties only occasionally draw much systematic attention. Analysis tends to concentrate on two major sets of issues. One is the question of state behavior. How do we understand the policies of national governments in the global economy? The other is the question of system governance. How do states cope with the consequences of economic interdependence? These two issues constitute what, in formal language, may be called the American school's core "problematique."

In principle, three broad levels of analysis are distinguished, each a general theoretical orientation corresponding to one of the well-known "images" of IR initially sketched by theorist Kenneth Waltz. In his classic *Man, the State, and War* (1959), Waltz sought to categorize the causes of war in as concise a fashion as possible. Any possible *casus belli*, he suggested could usefully be ordered under one of three headings: (1) within individuals; (2) within individual states; or (3) within the structure of the inter-state system. The first of his three images stressed defects in human nature; the second, defects in the internal organization of states; and the third, defects in states' external organization (the anarchic inter-state system). Today these are referred to, respectively, as the first, second, and third images of IR.

In practice, most attention in the American school is directed toward the systemic and domestic levels of analysis and the interaction between them. As two noted US scholars put it some years back in an authoritative survey: "The most challenging questions in IPE have to do with the interaction of domestic and international factors as they affect economic policies and outcomes ... [We] need to take into account both the domestic political economy of foreign economic policy and the role of strategic interaction among nation-states" (Frieden and Martin 2002: 119–20). The field's cutting edge, they said, is the "international-domestic research frontier." The style was codified subsequently by David Lake – a former president of both the American Political Science Association and the International Studies Association – under the label Open Economy Politics (OEP). For the American school, Lake declared, the synthesis of second- and third-image analysis is the "dominant approach [that] now structures and guides research" (Lake 2006: 757). In US-style IPE, the international-domestic frontier is where the action is.

OEP, as Lake summarized it, is largely materialist in orientation and builds outward in linear fashion from the micro to the macro: from the interests of individuals and other social units at the domestic level to policy preferences and strategic interactions at the international level. For analytical purposes, the paradigm is decomposed into a sequence of three steps. First come individuals or groups – e.g., firms, sectors, or factors of production – that can reasonably be assumed to share more or less the same material interests, defined as preferences over alternative outcomes. Interests are derived from established economic theories that highlight the distributional implications of different national policies. Next, OEP turns to how interests are aggregated and mediated through domestic political institutions. Drawing on familiar models from political science, the approach theorizes how divergent interests may be translated through political processes into public policy. Finally, once policy preferences are determined, OEP assumes a stage of international bargaining as states seek to influence one another's behavior, either explicitly or implicitly. At issue are the distributional consequences of alternative joint outcomes across states. Each state is naturally assumed to seek the best deal it can.

The strength of the OEP paradigm lies in the care it takes to delineate the microfoundations of government policy. A key weakness is its heavy reliance on formal theory and strict empirical methods, which together tend to drain much of the color of real life from analysis. American-style IPE is not alone in this respect. The fault is shared by many other social science specialties as well – not least the modern discipline of economics, with all its notorious emphasis on mathematics and models. Dissatisfaction among economists with their discipline's love of abstractions is widespread. A prime example is provided by the Nobel laureate Robert Shiller (2019), who suggests that his colleagues in the dismal science need to use a more commonsense approach to worldly events: more recourse to complex narratives that go beyond what technical models alone can measure. "My argument," he writes, "is that economists can best advance their *science* by developing and incorporating into it the *art* of narrative economics" (Shiller 2019: xxi; emphasis in the original). Sadly, however, the trend in economics appears, if anything, to be going the other way. In Shiller's words (2019: 12): the discipline "has lagged behind most other disciplines in attending to the importance of narratives." And even more sadly, much the same may be said as well of the American school of IPE, which as I have suggested elsewhere has fallen victim over time to a kind of "creeping economism" (Cohen 2008: 43).

The OEP paradigm is also weakened by its credulous deference to theories borrowed from economics and political science, some of which actually are quite dated. In intellectual terms, that dilutes much of OEP's claim to originality. As one colleague has suggested to me, it would not be particularly unfair to say that the paradigm "is nothing more than a combination of other ideas, an 'applier' rather than an 'innovator.'" Worse, the models that are used in the approach may be mutually contradictory, at odds with one another. Analytical conclusions may vary widely depending on what is initially assumed. Consider, for example, the question of trade preferences. Many studies rely on the familiar Heckscher–Ohlin factor-endowments theory, now a century old, and its corollary the Stolper–Samuelson theorem, to establish the distributional implications of alternative trade policies (Hiscox 2001). Political cleavages are defined in terms of class interests: capital versus labor. But, then, what about the Ricardo–Viner model, also quite dated, which defines cleavages in terms of industries, or the so-called "new" trade theory of the 1980s that defines interests in terms of firm size (Madeira 2014)? And what about the effect of non-materialist considerations, such as the sociotropic preferences stressed by Edward Mansfield, a political economist, and Diana Mutz, a social psychologist (Mansfield and Mutz 2009)? Each new twist produces a different conclusion. In a survey of 25 years of empirical OEP-style scholarship on trade policy, Thomas Oatley, a well-known US scholar, reached the "rather disappointing conclusion [that] individual findings have not produced consensus on any of the major questions at the center of research" (Oatley 2017: 699). In a parallel review of the IPE of money, I reached much the same judgment (Cohen 2017).

Perhaps the biggest weakness of OEP is its choice to study policymaking from the inside out, largely in isolation from broader macro processes – a striking form of methodological reductionism. Feedback effects from the outside in are not necessarily excluded. Even as he codified the approach, Lake acknowledged the possibility of external influences in the form of market power or international organizations but discounted their significance. In his words, "they do not challenge the hard core of the paradigm" (Lake 2009: 232). Typically, causation is assumed to run overwhelmingly in just one direction, from domestic preferences and institutions (steps one and two) to international outcomes (step three); the possibility of inverse outside-in influences tends to be downplayed or ignored. Oatley (2011), in a frequently cited paper, calls this the "reductionist gamble" – a risky bet that results attained by reducing analysis to the driving force of domestic politics will not be moderated or distorted by developments at the international level. More recent scholarship acknowledges that in many cases the reductionist gamble may indeed miss important interactions between the international and domestic levels of analysis (Chaudoin et al. 2015).

Newer empirical studies are careful to note the extent to which causation may in run in both directions, outside-in as well as inside-out. A prime example is provided by two well-known US scholars, Henry Farrell and Abraham Newman, in their so-called "new interdependence approach" to IPE, which focuses on the role of reciprocal rule overlaps between national jurisdictions together with power asymmetries among states to explain policy outcomes (Farrell and Newman 2016). Another example comes from a pair of younger scholars (Kim and Margalit 2021) in a study of the trade conflict between the United States and China instigated by Donald Trump during his term as President. In response to Trump's aggressive tariffs on imports from China, their research reveals, retaliatory tariffs by the Chinese government systematically targeted US goods that had production concentrated in Republican-supporting electoral districts. The aim, apparently successful, was to push voters to turn against Republican candidates – a clear instance of outside-in influence. In the words of the two researchers: "These findings demonstrate how domestic political institutions can be a source of vulnerability in interstate disputes" (Kim and Margalit 2021: 1).

Scholars working in the orthodox IPE tradition have applied the OEP paradigm to virtually every issue facing governments in the world economy – trade policy, monetary and financial relations, foreign direct investment, migration, foreign aid, natural resources, and environmental policy, to name just the most obvious. Collectively, within its state-centric ontology, the American school's agenda knows few bounds. Individual contributions, however, are typically more modest – what might be described as "small-bore" in caliber – focusing on just bits of the scene rather than the whole. In technical language, analysis tends to be partial-equilibrium (holding many variables constant) rather than general-equilibrium in nature. Some discussions assume interests that are given in order to study how different domestic institutions aggregate or refract preferences under varying circumstances. Others set aside the complexities of domestic politics in order to isolate the direct impact of constituency preferences on policy. And yet others may simply assume a set of policy interests at the state level in order to evaluate the dynamics of international bargaining.

In principle, nothing stands in the way of a more general-equilibrium approach that would bind the components together into a more complete whole. But as Lake (2009: 225) has ruefully acknowledged, "in practice synthesis remains imperfect." Theorizing, for the most part, remains determinedly micro- or mid-level.

Variations

Theorizing, however, is by no means monolithic. Quite the contrary, in fact. The American school does not lack for within-type variance. Adherents largely agree on the need for a state-centric ontology, with an emphasis on positivism and empiricism; they concur as well on what constitutes the fundamental problematique for analysis. Yet there is also much disagreement on more specific questions, reflecting broad debates that have gone on among IR theorists for years. Orthodoxy, in practice, encompasses many variations – a multiplicity of traditions that can all claim a degree of intellectual legitimacy (Cohen 2009).

Perhaps the deepest split is the classic divide between *liberalism* and *realism* in mainstream IR theory. Of the many issues that separate these two historical schools of thought, the most fundamental has to do with the nature of the underlying connection between economic and political activity. This is an age-old question that has been long contested by scholars of political economy. Does economics drive politics, or vice

versa? Central to the many versions of liberalism (later, neoliberal insti-
tutionalism) is a belief that economics dominates politics – meaning, in
particular, the forces of market competition and incentives for material
advancement. Variants of realism (later neorealism), by contrast, have
always retained faith in the capacity of political factors – especially
the distribution of power among states – to shape economic structures.
Correspondingly, realists have always favored the systemic level of analysis, where power and politics are central. Liberals, on the other hand, are
more comfortable with the domestic level of analysis, where economic
factors mold the constellations of interests that are assumed to be at the
heart of the policy process.

In time, the differences between liberalism and realism have come
to seem less crucial than their similarities – in particular, their effective
convergence around what John Ruggie (1999: 215), a senior US scholar,
has called "neo-utilitarian precepts and premises." Both traditions share
a preference for a purely rationalist, materialist, and individualistic
approach to analysis (utilitarianism). Actors, whether states or non-state
entities, are assumed to act in pursuit of clearly defined interests, usually
expressed in terms of tangible preferences and goals. Identities in
a rational-actor model are well established and unchanging. Outcomes
reflect a careful balancing of the material costs and benefits of alternative paths of behavior. Today, by contrast, some of the most vigorous
debates are between neo-utilitarianism of any kind and *cognitive* analysis
(first-image analysis), which rests on a logic of appropriateness rather
than a logic of material consequence. Collectively, cognitive approaches
go under the broad label of *constructivism*, with roots in either psychology or sociology.

On the psychology side, constructivist research highlights the role of
innate beliefs and biases. In place of a pure rational-actor model, emphasis is placed on emotions, ideas, and the cognitive short cuts that are often
used in the policy process. Recent work along these lines has borrowed
from the newly fashionable branch of economics known as behavioral
economics, which demonstrates how such concepts as framing, loss aversion, fairness, and myopic time horizons help to explain state behavior.
On the sociology side, research highlights the role of social relations in
determining actor perceptions of identity and interests. In place of the
autonomous individual, emphasis is placed on intersubjective understandings and the development of social norms. Prominent in scholarship
of this type is a growing literature incorporating core elements of feminist theory. Traditional neo-utilitarian approaches, feminists contend,

are innately androcentric, owing to the early dominance of the field by men (with the notable exception of Susan Strange). Dominant ideas in the field reflect masculine identities that were socially constructed from birth. Conventional analysis, therefore, is inherently biased, favoring male perspectives and interests. Research that neglects the role of gender is bound to yield a distorted understanding of how the global economy actually works.

Most recently, ambitious attempts have been made to synthesize elements of neo-utilitarianism and constructivism into a single framework intended to help understand the evolution of the global economic system through time. Prominent examples include *Economic Ideas in Political Time*, a book by Wesley Widmaier (2016), and "Black Swans, Lame Ducks, and the Mystery of IPE's Missing Macroeconomy," an article by Blyth and Matthijs (2017). Both systematically explore the vital role that ideas may play, through their interaction with political and social institutions, in explaining the rise and fall of international economic orders.

HETERODOX PERSPECTIVES

Heterodox ("radical" or "critical") perspectives differ from orthodoxy in terms of any or all of our five defining attributes. Ontology tends to be less state-centric; agendas, broader and more normative; disciplinary boundaries, more open; and methodology, less formal. Indeed, as the label of heterodoxy implies, theoretical approaches often define themselves explicitly in contradistinction to orthodoxy – opposed, in particular, to the conventions of the "mainstream" American style. In an earlier iteration (Cohen 2008), I compared the American school directly with what I chose to call the British school. Subsequent discussion, however, has made clear that the dominant style of IPE in the UK is not exclusive to the British Isles. Much is shared in common with heterodox perspectives to be found elsewhere around the globe, including in the US (Cohen 2019). The umbrella of heterodoxy is very wide.

But here too diversity rules. Heterodox approaches also come in many flavors – many competing variations on a set of common themes. In fact, within-type variance is, at times, extreme.

Common Themes

Five themes stand out, to a greater or lesser extent, to broadly distinguish heterodox perspectives from orthodoxy, corresponding to our five defining attributes.

First is a rejection of the state-centrism of the American style. States still matter, but so too do many other units of analysis, ranging from the individual to the global. The state is just one actor of interest among many, and by no means the most central. Michael Zürn, a noted German scholar, speaks of the "analytical shackles of 'methodological nationalism,'" which "considers nation-states as the basic unit of all politics" (Zürn 2013: 416). Heterodoxy scorns the restraints of a narrow focus on national governments that automatically exclude alternative ways of thinking about the world. Heterodox approaches question why the state must necessarily be prioritized for purposes of analysis. For the American school, with its roots in the discipline of political science, a focus on the sovereign nation seems natural. But for others, coming to the subject from other academic specialties such as sociology, history, or global studies, other ontologies seem equally legitimate. The shackles of methodological nationalism, says heterodoxy, must be shed.

Second is a broadening of the research agenda to go well beyond orthodoxy's core problematique of inter-state politics and governance. For many heterodox scholars, it makes sense to concentrate instead on the evolution of the global system as a whole, understood in terms of vast and complex social structures, with particular emphasis on transcendent issues of power, inequality, development, and change. The core problematique, it is argued, should encompass the causes and consequences of systemic transformation in historical context – what one sympathizer has labeled a "historical-relativist paradigm" (Tooze 1985: 121). A wide-band historical-relativist paradigm contrasts sharply with the more granular focus of the American school, where broader structures are rarely problematized.

Third is a departure from strictly positive analysis, with its emphasis on objectivity in research. Most heterodox approaches tend to be more normative in ambition. Scholarship tends to be critical of established orthodoxies and more engaged with social issues, impatient with the status quo, and more eager to change attitudes or practices. The world-view is anything but dispassionate. The perspective is ecumenical, concerned with all manner of societal and ethical issues. The main purpose of research is judgment: to identify injustice. Where the mainstream

American school aspires to the lofty impartiality of conventional US social science, heterodox approaches tend to be more openly value driven in the tradition of classical moral philosophy. Fourth is a greater receptivity to academic specialties other than economics and political science in the spirit of the open range advocated by Strange. Inspiration is drawn from a variety of disciplines, from sociology and history to anthropology and geography. For heterodox scholars, IPE is about much more than simply the pursuit of material wealth or the processes of public governance. It is about society as a whole – with all its multiple disharmonies and complexities. So why limit ourselves to just what economics or political science can teach us? Analysis should seek illumination from wherever it can be found, regardless of traditional disciplinary boundaries

Fifth, finally, is a more relaxed attitude toward analytical methods. Epistemology takes second place to purpose. Scholarship tends to be more qualitative than in the orthodox American style, attaching less importance to narrow hypothesis testing or systematic sifting of granulated evidence. Theorizing, instead, is typically more interpretive in tone and more institutional and historical in nature – more in the spirit of Robert Shiller's "narrative economics," adding art to science. The formalism of hypothetico-deductivism is valued less than a broad organic interpretation of the social context of IPE. Where the American school tends to be ahistorical, implicitly or explicitly assuming a static framework for analytical purposes, heterodox approaches take time more directly into account. And where the American school self-consciously restricts itself mainly to mid-level theorizing, heterodox approaches tend to aim for grander visions of structural transformation or social development. The central goal is to come to grips with the great issues of life.

However, for all that heterodox approaches have in common, they are no more monolithic than orthodoxy – perhaps even less so. Here too perspectives come in many flavors, reflecting sharp disagreements over all kinds of more specific questions. The field of IPE is strewn with battles among competing heterodox visions. At the risk of oversimplification – and acknowledging again that any system of classification is bound to be, to some degree, arbitrary – it is possible to group most heterodox approaches roughly into three related sub-categories: system-level theories, critical theory, and a medley of more specialized contributions that seek to extend the boundaries of the field in one direction or another.

SYSTEM-LEVEL THEORIES

System-level theories are distinguished by their ontology, which centers on global structures and processes. The basic unit of interest is nothing less than the world as a whole. The aim is to understand systemic transformation – how and why global orders change over time. The preferred mode of analysis is a historical-relativist paradigm.

Marxism

Oldest among heterodox system-level perspectives is, of course, classical Marxism – the intellectual tradition tracing back to the writings of Karl Marx in the nineteenth century. As a body of theory, Marxism means, above all, a commitment to "historical materialism," which Marx defined as the "materialist conception of history." The materialism in historical materialism means placing economic relations and the social organization of production (the "modes" of production) at the very center of analysis, with particular emphasis on the inherent "contradictions" of capitalism and the "commodification" of all aspects of life. Marx himself had remarkably little to say about the international dimension of political economy. But building on his original insights, subsequent generations of his disciples have used the lens of a historical-relativist paradigm to construct a theoretical perspective, centering on class relations, that claims to provide a definitive explanation of the world economy's underlying dynamics. For those working in the Marxist tradition today, such as William Robinson in the United States (2014), Leo Panitch in Canada (2008), Ben Selwyn in Britain (2015), or Bastiaan van Apeldoorn in the Netherlands (2014), there is no difference between the global system and global capitalism. The global system *is* global capitalism. The focus of IPE, therefore, should properly be on the "laws of motion" of contemporary capitalism.

Dependency Theory

Over time, the intellectual tradition bequeathed by Marx has proved to be a source of inspiration for a wide range of alternative system-level approaches, each combining elements of Marxist analysis with other ideas to offer its own heterodox vision of how the world works. One of the first of these was dependency theory, a school of thought that first emerged in Latin America in the 1950s seeking to explain the persistent poverty of peripheral regions around the globe. Long before, Marxist theorists had already promoted the image of a stratified world economy divided between a dominant core and a dependent periphery, extrapolating from V.I. Lenin's 1917 polemic, *Imperialism, the Highest Stage of Capitalism*. Global capitalism, according to Leninist ideology, naturally degenerates into a system of economic imperialism – rich nations exploiting the poor. With this image in mind, dependency theory added new insights about the constraints that allegedly bar improvements in the periphery. Dependency, it was argued, was self-perpetuating, brutally imposed by the prevailing structure of economic relations and offering no easy escape. Inequality was not just an accident of history. Rather, it was intrinsic, an inherent product of the periphery's dependent role in the global division of labor. Prevailing capitalist structures systematically deformed local economies and bound them to their fate – the "development of underdevelopment," as Andre Gunder Frank (1966), a leading *dependentista*, later put it. Dependency theory remains popular today among scholars in less advanced economies, such as Brazil's Alexandre Rands Borros (2017) or Nigeria's Luke Amadi (2012).

World-Systems Theory

Another system-level perspective inspired in part by Marxism is world-systems theory, which also focuses on the causes and consequences of stratification in the global economy. World-systems theory grew out of the writings of the sociologist Immanuel Wallerstein, starting with the first volume of a monumental multivolume treatise on *The Modern World-System* published in 1974 (Wallerstein 1974). Subsequent volumes were published in 1980, 1989, and 2011. Like Marxist IPE, world-systems theory concentrates on the evolution of the global capitalist system, but without the rigors of Leninist ideology.

Generically, world-systems are conceived as comprehensive human interaction networks, encompassing everything from the individual and households to national and global markets. The specific system that prevails today, the *modern* world-system, has origins that date back to the sixteenth century. The modern world-system is understood as a hierarchical and long-lasting structure composed of three distinct tiers: a dominant core along with dependent peripheral and semi-peripheral regions. Capitalism is assumed to contribute to the dynamics of the modern world-system, but only in part. Important as well is geopolitics, where corporations and governments compete vigorously for power and wealth. Competition among firms and states, in turn, is conditioned by an ongoing struggle among social classes and by the resistance of peripheral and semi-peripheral peoples to domination and exploitation from the core. No political center exists compared to past imperial systems like the Roman Empire.

To earlier Marxist characterizations of the global system Wallerstein added much nuance, including the fresh notion of a semi-periphery that mediates between the other two tiers. Found in the semi-periphery are the larger countries of the developing world such as Brazil or India, along with other smaller countries at an intermediate level of development such as Chile, Thailand, and Turkey. While the core enjoys a high level of technological development, selling sophisticated high-value goods and services, the role of the periphery is to supply raw materials, foodstuffs, and cheap labor on a basis of unequal exchange. Between them, the semi-periphery benefits from exploiting the periphery even as it is itself exploited by the core.

Following Wallerstein, others have added their own twist to world-systems theory. Representative is Christopher Chase-Dunn, a long-time proponent of the perspective. In 1989 Chase-Dunn published *Global Formation: Structures of the World Economy* (1989), a major synthesis and restatement of Wallerstein's legacy, which has since become a standard reference for others working in the same vein. The world-systems perspective is especially popular with sociologists and other students of social change, providing a direct counterpoint to the mainstream American school of IPE. Institutional support is provided by the Political Economy of the World-System section of the American Sociological Association. A substantial number of world-systems theorists are located in the US, such as Robert Denemark, another long-time proponent (Denemark 2021), and Jason Moore, an environmental historian who has developed his own "world-ecology" approach to the subject (Moore 2015).

World Orders

Elsewhere, another counterpoint at the system level was provided by the pioneering contributions of Robert Cox, a Canadian, who was also driven by a commitment to historical materialism to think in terms of a succession of complex social structures defined by their modes of production. He too had in mind a historical-relativist paradigm. But in place of the rigid stratifications characteristic of dependency theory or world-systems theory, Cox proposed a more fluid concept that he chose to call "world orders" – a succession of global systems that he saw as a function of three broad influences: material capabilities, ideas, and institutions. Historical change, he insisted, had to be thought of in terms of the reciprocal relationship of structures and actors within a much broader conceptualization of international relations, the "state-society complex." Outcomes would depend on the actions of "social forces," defined as the main collective actors engendered by the relations of production both within and across all spheres of activity. "International production," he wrote, "is mobilizing social forces, and it is through these forces that its major political consequences *vis-à-vis* the nature of states and future world orders may be anticipated" (Cox 1981: 147). The overriding imperative, he insisted, was to support social forces that would "bargain for a better deal within the world economy" (Cox 1981: 151).

Cox's theories, encouraging interpretative historical analysis, have shaped generations of scholarship since they were first articulated in the early 1980s. Though largely ignored by the American school, his writings are still widely taught and debated in Britain as well as in Canada, his homeland. "The work of Robert Cox," remarks one British observer, "has inspired many students to rethink the way in which we study international political economy, and it is fair to say that [his] historical materialism is perhaps the most important alternative to realist and liberal perspectives in the field today" (Griffiths 1999: 118). Another influential scholar, a Canadian based in Europe, describes the study of Cox's state-society complex as "*the* problem of international political economy" (Underhill 2006: 16; emphasis in the original). To this day, numerous sources cite Cox as the starting point for their own theoretical contributions. In a recent volume of essays promoting heterodox perspectives in IPE, Cox is cited reverently by almost every contributor (Shields et al. 2011).

CRITICAL THEORY

Heterodoxy's second sub-category is critical theory, ambitiously conceived as a form of inquiry aimed at attaining nothing less than general human emancipation. In the words of one sympathetic commentary, "Critical IPE scholars do not mince words about the normative ambitions of their scholarship" (Kranke 2014: 898). Their agenda is the broadest possible. Their goal is to decrease domination and increase autonomy in all its forms. Though the approach overlaps with system-level theories, it also encompasses other levels of analysis down to social units as small as the family or the firm. At every level, declares a trio of critical theorists, "the purpose of our knowledge is to further human freedom" (van Apeldoorn et al. 2011: 218).

Critical theory is distinguished by two related assumptions. First, empirical research cannot be separated from normative inquiry. Any notion that actors and processes in IPE can be treated in strictly objective terms is rejected. Rather, forms of agency must be understood as historically and socially dynamic and mutually constituted. And second, socioeconomic and political structures must be problematized. They are not neutral categories, given and immutable. Rather, they are potentially transitory and subject to evolutionary or revolutionary change.

Given the breadth of its ambition, critical theory is not easily summarized. Encompassed within the category are diverse variations on Marxist themes as well as all kinds of other heterodox schools of thought. As one exponent acknowledges, "There is no neat definition of what constitutes critical political economy" (Dunn 2020: 1). As a result, infighting among factions is not uncommon. While some see critical theory as blossoming (Cafruny et al. 2016), others insist sadly that "critical IPE has entered into a process of sclerosis" (Belfrage and Worth 2012: 132). I remember long ago reading a critique of battles among Marxist factions, which in a memorable phrase was likened to "vicious little beasts devouring one another in a drop of water." (Decades later, I cannot trace the source.) At times, that seems a fitting description of critical theory.

Yet there remain ties that bind. One sympathetic source suggests that a more adequate label for critical theory would be "ideologically oriented inquiry" (Griffiths 1999: 114). The common denominator, according to another commentary, is an "oppositional frame of mind" (Brown 2001: 192). Critical theory challenges orthodoxies of every sort and is particularly averse to modern capitalism in all its guises. Critical theorists may not agree on what they are for, but they surely know what they are against. As a placard in a London May Day demonstration once proclaimed: "Capitalism should be replaced by something nicer."

EXTENSIONS

Finally, we come to a sub-category of more specialized contributions that seek to formally extend the boundaries of the field in one direction or another. The motive for these innovations is a sense that something important is missing from the path that scholarship has followed until now. The aim is to interpolate insights from other specialties in order to point research toward a fresh conception of IPE's ontology and purpose. The change is typically signaled by the addition of a novel descriptive label for the field.

For instance, a Historical IPE – HIPE – was advocated some years back by Paul Langley, an eminent British scholar, who called for the field to "look to history as an anchor from which to construct knowledge of the international political economy" (Langley 2002: 10). The boundaries of the field should be extended to fully incorporate "social time" as a "principal category for inquiry" (Langley 2002: 10). A case for the extension was made by contrasting the proposed HIPE with mainstream orthodoxy, which we know tends to be mostly ahistorical in its framing of issues. But among heterodox perspectives, system-level approaches had already long put history front and center, even without the added adjective; the boundaries of the field had already been extended to incorporate the dynamics of time. In practice, Langley was pushing against an open door. IPE, at least for heterodox scholars, was already historical. Few have seen the need to use the label HIPE instead.

An even broader emphasis on history has been promoted more recently by John M. Hobson, another British scholar. Hobson argues for supplanting today's "Eurocentric" IPE, rooted as it is in Western experience and perspectives, with a much wider take acknowledging the role that other parts of the world have played in the development of the field. His preferred label is either Inter-Civilizational Political Economy (Hobson 2013) or New Global Political Economy (Hobson 2021). The important contributions of early non-Western thinkers have also been emphasized by Eric Helleiner (2020), a leading Canadian scholar.

For other scholars, what is needed is a more comparative take on IPE, dissolving what is regarded as a false dichotomy between international (or global) political economy and comparative political economy (Clift et al. 2021). Many researchers, especially on the European continent, call for a new Comparative Historical Political Economy (Boettke et al. 2013). The roots of CHPE go back to the work of the British researchers Peter Hall and David Soskice (2001), who popularized the study of comparative national capitalisms (captured in the phrase "varieties of capitalism"). What distinguishes CHPE is a shift of focus to the international level of analysis. The aim is to develop a set of analytical tools that could be used to compare historical phases of global capitalism. But these variants too have so far failed to develop much traction in the field.

More successful has been a lively movement among heterodox scholars aiming to extend analysis to incorporate a more sociological conception of the field. The movement has been given the name Everyday IPE – EIPE (Hobson and Seabrooke 2009). The label signifies a shift from formal politics to a much greater emphasis on the dynamics of underlying social relations, both domestic and transnational. The proposed view is strictly "bottom up." Most theoretical approaches, whether orthodox or heterodox, focus on elite "power makers," whether they be hegemonic powers, international institutions, the capitalist class, or politicians. With EIPE, the spotlight turns to everyday folk, society's diverse masses of "power takers." Through their routine daily practices and patterns of behavior, non-elite actors can confer or withhold legitimacy from elite dictates and thus exercise an independent influence on outcomes. An excellent example is provided by Kate Bedford, a British scholar, in her prize-winning study of British bingo halls and their impact on systems of regulation (Bedford 2019). It may have been a bit premature to declare EIPE "a new and emergent school of IPE," as one prominent source did when the idea was first broached (Blyth 2009: 18). But it is clear that the proposed approach has added a fresh and distinctive take on what the field is all about.

Notable more recently has been a phalanx of theorists calling for a new cultural turn in IPE, comparable to the rise of constructivism as a challenge to neo-utilitarianism on the other side of the orthodox/heterodox divide. Cultural IPE seeks to highlight the importance of the cognitive level of analysis as a complement to more traditional rationalist and materialist approaches. At issue, in particular, is the question of identity, which provides a system of meaning through which social life is both interpreted and organized. Culture, two leading exponents write, "is simultaneously homogenizing – as one means by which people in specific settings come to develop a sense of shared identity through common interpretations of similar phenomena – and differentiating – as a means of distinguishing different cultures through the meanings they attribute to different things" (Best and Paterson 2010: 7). Without due consideration for the role that culture plays in shaping social behavior, advocates argue, analysis is necessarily incomplete.

Also notable has been a parallel movement, likewise inspired at least in part by the rise of constructivism, that aims to make gender studies an integral part of the field – a feminist IPE (Bakker 2007). At issue for feminist scholars are the gendered meanings that we attach to different kinds of economic activity. Traditional neo-utilitarian perspectives implicitly tend to value so-called masculine activities (e.g., competing, making money) more highly than activities commonly thought of as feminine (e.g., reproduction, family care). Hierarchies, therefore, tend to be gendered and to work to the disadvantage of women. The challenge is to highlight how understandings of masculinity and femininity shape behavior and outcomes. The solution is to bring gender into the core of analysis as a key causal variable. In the words of one leading advocate, "feminist work is not a digression from nor supplement to conventional accounts; rather, it is an *essential orientation* for advancing our theory *and* practice of political economy" (Peterson 2005: 518; emphasis in the original).

Yet another extension has been prompted by concerns about climate change and its attendant impacts (Katz-Rosene et al. 2021). The global environment, it is argued, can no longer be relegated to the margins of the field. The dangers of global warming and the decline of biodiversity are simply too great to be ignored. Damage is speeding up all around us. Greenhouse gas emissions continue to grow; temperatures continue to increase; the oceans are acidifying; species extinction is spreading; permafrosts are melting; the rainforests are disappearing; hurricanes and floods are becoming more numerous and intense – all part of what earth scientists call the "great acceleration." A new Global Ecological Political Economy (GEPE), we are told, is needed to explore how all of this will shape the future of the world economy (Katz-Rosene and Paterson 2018). Nothing less than the survival of the human species may be at stake.

Lastly, we have a new Political Economy of Complex Interdependence – PECI – that has recently been proposed by Oatley (2019). Connectivity in the world economy, Oatley argues, has grown beyond the capacity of existing theoretical models. Today's increasingly complex interdependence demands that we draw on formal complexity theories from the natural sciences as well as information theory to fully understand the global system. As Oatley puts it: "PECI conceptualizes the global political economy as a complex system ... a structure of relationships that stretches within and spans across societies and whose dynamic characteristics are such as to generate unexpected outcomes" (Oatley 2019: 961). It is clear that the approach contrasts sharply with the OEP paradigm, which Oatley uses as a point of comparison. But it is less clear how much substantive difference there is from already established heterodox approaches like world-systems theory or Cox's world orders. How much real value is added, accordingly, is an open question. Whether or to what extent PECI catches on as a distinct extension of the field remains to be seen.

CONCLUSION

In summary, it appears that a Big Picture of IPE is indeed possible despite the dense proliferation of trees in the forest. Our five defining attributes – ontology, agenda, purpose, boundaries, and epistemology – help us to make sense of all the cacophony. A concise taxonomy is provided in Appendix A. The Big Picture tells us what specialists have come to think about the character and boundaries of the modern field after more than a half-century of development. The question now is: Can we rethink IPE?

REFERENCES

Amadi, Luke (2012), "Africa, Beyond the New Dependency: A Political Economy," *African Journal of Political Science and International Relations* 6:8, 191–203.

Bakker, Isabella (2007), "Social Reproduction and the Constitution of a Gendered Political Economy," *New Political Economy* 12:4, 541–56.

Bedford, Kate (2019), *Bingo Capitalism: The Law and Political Economy of Everyday Gambling* (New York: Oxford University Press).

Belfrage, Claes and Owen Worth (2012), "Critical International Political Economy: Renewing Critique and Ontologies," *International Politics* 49:2, 131–5.

Best, Jacqueline and Matthew Paterson (2010), "Introduction: Understanding Cultural Political Economy," in Jacqueline Best and Matthew Paterson, eds., *Cultural Political Economy* (New York: Routledge), 1–25.

Blyth, Mark (2009), "Introduction: IPE as a Global Conversation," in Mark Blyth, ed., *Routledge Handbook of International Political Economy (IPE): IPE as a Global Conversation* (London: Routledge), 1–20.

Blyth, Mark and Matthias Matthijs (2017), "Black Swans, Lame Ducks, and the Mystery of IPE's Missing Macroeconomy," *Review of International Political Economy* 24:2, 203–31.

Boettke, Peter J., Christopher J. Coyne, and Peter T. Leseson (2013), "Comparative Historical Political Economy," *Journal of Institutional Economics* 9:3, 285–301.

Borros, Alexandre Rands (2017), *Roots of Brazilian Relative Economic Backwardness* (Amsterdam: Elsevier).

Brown, Chris (2001), "Our Side? Critical Theory and International Relations," in R.W. Jones, ed., *Critical Theory and World Politics* (Boulder, CO: Lynne Rienner), 191–204.

Cafruny, Alan W., Gonzalo Pozo Martin, and Leila Simona Talani (2016), "Introduction," in Alan W. Cafruny, Leila Simona Talani, and Gonzalo Pozo

Martin, eds., *Palgrave Handbook of Critical International Political Economy* (London: Palgrave Macmillan), 1–6.

Chase-Dunn, Christopher K. (1989), *Global Formation: Structures of the World Economy* (New York: Basic Blackwell).

Chaudoin, Steven, Helen V. Milner, and Xun Pang (2015), "International Systems and Domestic Politics: Linking Complex Interactions with Empirical Models in International Relations," *International Organization* 69:2, 275–309.

Clift, Ben, Peter M. Kristensen, and Ben Rosamond (2021), "Remembering and Forgetting IPE: Disciplinary History as Boundary Work," *Review of International Political Economy* (forthcoming).

Cohen, Benjamin J. (2008), *International Political Economy: An Intellectual History* (Princeton, NJ: Princeton University Press).

Cohen, Benjamin J. (2009), "The Multiple Traditions of American IPE," in Mark Blyth, ed., *Routledge Handbook of International Political Economy (IPE): IPE as a Global Conversation* (London: Routledge), 23–35.

Cohen, Benjamin J. (2017), "The IPE of Money Revisited," *Review of International Political Economy* 24:4, 657–80.

Cohen, Benjamin J. (2019), *Advanced Introduction to International Political Economy*, 2nd edition (Cheltenham, UK and Northampton, MA, USA: Edward Elgar Publishing).

Cox, Robert (1981), "Social Forces, States, and World Orders: Beyond International Relations Theory," *Millennium* 10:2, 126–55.

Denemark, Robert A. (2021), "Uneven and Combined Development, International Political Economy, and World-Systems Analysis," *Cambridge Review of International Affairs*, DOI: 10.1080/09557571.2021.1889972.

Dunn, Bill (2020), "What Makes Critical Research in Political Economy?" in Bill Dunn, ed., *A Research Agenda for Critical Political Economy* (Cheltenham, UK and Northampton, MA, USA: Edward Elgar Publishing), 1–18.

Farrell, Henry and Abraham Newman (2016), "The New Interdependence Approach: Theoretical Developments and Empirical Demonstration," *Review of International Political Economy* 23:5, 713–36.

Frank, Andre Gunder (1966), *The Development of Underdevelopment* (New York: Monthly Review Press).

Frieden, Jeffry A. and Lisa L. Martin (2002), "International Political Economy: Global and Domestic Interactions," in Ira Katznelson and Helen V. Milner, eds., *Political Science: State of the Discipline* (New York: Norton), 118–46.

Griffiths, Martin (1999), *Fifty Key Thinkers in International Relations* (New York: Routledge).

Hall, Peter and David Soskice (2001), *Varieties of Capitalism: The Institutional Foundations of Comparative Advantage* (New York: Oxford University Press).

Helleiner, Eric (2020), "Globalizing the Historical Roots of IPE," in Ernesto Vivares, ed., *The Routledge Handbook to Global Political Economy* (New York: Routledge), 43–57.

Hiscox, Michael (2001), "Class Versus Industry Cleavages: Inter-Industry Factor Mobility and the Politics of Trade," *International Organization* 55:1, 1–46.

Hobson, John M. (2013), "Part 2 – Reconstructing the Non-Eurocentric Foundations of IPE: From Eurocentric 'Open Economy Politics' to Inter-Civilizational Political Economy," *Review of International Political Economy* 20:5, 1055–81.

Hobson, John M. (2021), *Multicultural Origins of the Global Economy: Beyond the Western-Centric Frontier* (New York: Cambridge University Press).

Hobson, John M. and Leonard Seabrooke (2009), "Everyday International Political Economy," in Mark Blyth, ed., *Routledge Handbook of International Political Economy (IPE): IPE as a Global Conversation* (London: Routledge), 290–306.

Hveem, Helge (2011), "Pluralist IPE: A View from Outside the 'Schools,'" in Nicola Phillips and Catherine Weaver, eds., *International Political Economy: Debating the Past, Present and Future* (London: Routledge), 169–77.

Katz-Rosene, Ryan M. and Matthew Paterson (2018), *Thinking Ecologically about the Global Political Economy* (London: Routledge).

Katz-Rosene, Ryan M., Christopher Kelly-Bisson, and Matthew Paterson (2021), "Teaching Students to Think Ecologically about the Global Political Economy, and *Vice Versa*," *Review of International Political Economy* 28:4, 1083–98.

Kim, Sung Eun and Yotam Margalit (2021), "Tariffs as Electoral Weapons: The Political Geography of the US–China Trade War," *International Organization* 75:1, 1–38.

Kranke, Matthias (2014), "Which 'C' Are You Talking About? Critical Meets Cultural IPE," *Millennium*, 42:3, 897–907.

Lake, David A. (2006), "International Political Economy: A Maturing Interdiscipline," in Barry Weingast and D. Wittman, eds., *Oxford Handbook of Political Economy* (New York: Oxford University Press), 757–77.

Lake, David A. (2009), "Open Economy Politics: A Critical Review," *Review of International Organizations* 4:3, 219–44.

Langley, Paul (2002), *World Financial Orders: An Historical International Political Economy* (New York: Routledge).

Madeira, Mary Anne (2014), "The New Politics of the New Trade: The Political Economy of Intra-Industry Trade," in David A. Deese, ed., *Handbook of the International Political Economy of Trade* (Cheltenham, UK and Northampton, MA, USA: Edward Elgar Publishing), 113–34.

Mansfield, Edward and Diana Mutz (2009), "Support for Free Trade: Self-Interest, Sociotropic Politics, and Out-Group Anxiety," *International Organization* 63:3, 425–57.

Moore, Jason W. (2015), *Capitalism in the Web of Life: Ecology and the Accumulation of Capital* (London: Verso).

Oatley, Thomas H. (2011), "The Reductionist Gamble: Open Economy Politics in the Global Economy," *International Organization* 65:2, 311–41.

Oatley, Thomas H. (2017), "Open Economy Politics and Trade Policy," *Review of International Political Economy* 24:4, 699–717.

Oatley, Thomas H. (2019), "Toward a Political Economy of Complex Interdependence," *European Journal of International Relations* 25:4, 957–78.

Oatley, Thomas H. (2021), "Regaining Relevance: IPE and a Changing Global Political Economy," *Cambridge Review of International Affairs*, DOI: 10.1080/09557571.2021.1888880.

Panitch, Leo (2008), *Renewing Socialism: Transforming Democracy, Strategy and Imagination* (London: Merlin Press).

Peterson, V. Spike (2005), "How (the Meaning of) Gender Matters in Political Economy," *New Political Economy* 10:4, 499–521.

Ravenhill, John (2008), "In Search of the Missing Middle," *Review of International Political Economy* 15:1, 18–29.

Robinson, William I. (2014), *Global Capitalism and the Crisis of Humanity* (New York: Cambridge University Press).

Ruggie, John (1999), "What Makes the World Hang Together? Neo-utilitarianism and the Social Constructivist Challenge," in Peter Katzenstein, Robert Keohane, and Stephen Krasner, eds., *Exploration and Contestation in the Study of World Politics* (Cambridge, MA: The MIT Press), 215–45.

Seabrooke, Leonard and Kevin Young (2017), "The Networks and Niches of International Political Economy," *Review of International Political Economy* 24:2, 288–331.

Selwyn, Benjamin (2015), "Twenty-First-Century International Political Economy: A Class-Relational Perspective," *European Journal of International Relations* 21:3, 513–37.

Shields, Stuart, Ian Bruff, and Huw Macartney (2011), "Introduction: 'Critical' and 'International Political Economy,'" in Stuart Shields, Ian Bruff, and Huw Macartney, eds., *Critical International Political Economy: Dialogue, Debate and Dissensus* (London: Palgrave Macmillan), 1–6.

Shiller, Robert J. (2019), *Narrative Economics: How Stories Go Viral & Drive Major Economic Events* (Princeton, NJ: Princeton University Press).

Strange, Susan (1984), "Preface," in Susan Strange, ed., *Paths to International Political Economy* (London: George Allen & Unwin), ix–xi.

Strange, Susan (1991), "An Eclectic Approach," in Craig N. Murphy and Roger Tooze, eds., *The New International Political Economy* (Boulder, CO: Lynne Rienner), 33–49.

Tooze, Roger (1985), "International Political Economy," in Steve Smith, ed., *International Relations: British and American Perspectives* (Oxford: Basic Blackwell), 108–25.

Underhill, Geoffrey R.D. (2006), "Introduction: Conceptualizing the Changing Global Order," in Richard Stubbs and Geoffrey R.D. Underhill, eds., *Political Economy and the Changing Global Order*, 3rd edition (New York: Oxford University Press), 3–23.

van Apeldoorn, Bastiaan (2014), "The European Capitalist Class and the Crisis of its Hegemonic Project," *Socialist Register* 50, 189–206.

van Apeldoorn, Bastiaan, Ian Bruff, and Magnus Ryner (2011), "The Richness and Diversity of Critical IPE Perspectives: Moving Beyond the Debate on the 'British School,'" in Nicola Phillips and Catherine Weaver, eds., *International Political Economy: Debating the Past, Present and Future* (London: Routledge), 215–22.

Vivares, Ernesto, ed. (2020), *The Routledge Handbook to Global Political Economy* (New York: Routledge).

Wallerstein, Immanuel (1974), *The Modern World-System*, vol. 1 (New York: Academic Press).

Waltz, Kenneth (1959), *Man, the State, and War* (New York: Columbia University Press).

Widmaier, Wesley (2016), *Economic Ideas in Political Time* (Cambridge, UK: Cambridge University Press).

Zürn, Michael (2013), "Globalization and Global Governance," in Walter Carlsnaes, Thomas Risse, and Beth Simmons, eds., *Handbook of International Relations*, 2nd edition (London: Sage Publications), 401–25.

3. Rethinking purpose

Amidst all the cacophony of the Big Picture, the Why question is the most fundamental: Why do we study International Political Economy (IPE)? What is the purpose of it all? What do we hope to accomplish? In short, what is the field's *raison d'être*? Remarkably, for all the energy that individual scholars put into their work in IPE, little is said about what our collective goals are or should be. No wonder, then, that the field has drifted as much as it has. It is easy to go off course if you are unsure about where you want to go. It is time to rethink IPE's purpose.

POSSIBILITIES

The purpose of a field of study is by no means easy to summarize. To begin, purpose is to some extent subjective, a matter on which sincere individuals may sincerely disagree. Consensus is elusive. As one source put it years ago, "no answer that would be found acceptable by everyone can ... be given to the fundamental question about the purposes of study" (Reynolds 1987: 61). Worse, the collective goals of an area of inquiry may not even be formally articulated. They may add up to little more than a set of unspoken assumptions shared subliminally by a field's invisible college – a quiet intersubjective understanding of why the field exists and what it is meant to achieve. In other words, purpose may simply be taken for granted.

Whether articulated or not, however, there are only a few conceptions of purpose to choose from. One possibility might be labeled *professional advancement*. In practical terms, a field's main accomplishment may simply be to provide an opportunity for its diverse adherents to build a career pursuing their own personal interests. Research and publications may be seen primarily as a way to climb the ladder toward the top of the ivory tower. No broader collective goal may consciously motivate behavior. Such a possibility may seem cynical, of course, perhaps even selfish, but it cannot be dismissed out of hand. We all know that the academic life is highly rivalrous; there are only so many faculty appointments and other rewards to go around. Indeed, in many ways academia closely resembles Adam Smith's model of capitalism – self-interested individuals jointly producing something of general value under the guidance of the invisible hand of competition. Like it or not, we are all to some extent little capitalists relying on our reputation and fighting for market share.

But even admitting a role for self-interest it is rare that a field of study does not collectively aspire to some higher calling as well. Individual self-interest is like the cosmic microwave background (CMB) that astronomers tell us has permeated the universe since the original Big Bang some 14 billion years ago. The CMB provides a common context but does little to explain the many unique features observed out there in the cosmos. In the same way, self-interest can be assumed to be everywhere in the background of academic life, but on its own tells us little about how individuals in a field understand their joint purpose. For that, we must probe a bit deeper.

In the social sciences, three main possibilities present themselves. Understood as general archetypes, they are Comprehension, Critique, or Counsel. We may call them the three Cs.

Begin with *Comprehension*. For many social scientists, the main purpose of a field of study may simply be explanation – a better understanding of how the world works. Research is meant to be as objective as humanly possible, avoiding normative judgments about the prevailing social order. Emphasis is placed on accurate observation and interpretation of available empirical evidence. The ambition is to ferret out issue linkages and causal relationships that would appear in practice to govern behavior and drive outcomes. The intended audience is relatively narrow, primarily students and fellow scholars.

For many others, by contrast, mere comprehension is not enough. Research must be more in the style of *Critique* – more prepared to take sides, find fault, and in general challenge the status quo. Emphasis is placed on revealing deep defects in existing social structures. The ambition, ultimately, is disruption – to promote radical and far-reaching change at a broad systemic level. The intended audience is anyone hoping to make the world a nicer place to live.

And for yet others, a field's main purpose might be *Counsel* – to offer practical advice about persistent or emerging social problems. The field is seen as more than just a conversation among scholars. It should also be a venue for applied professional skills. Research ought to be directly useful to relevant decision makers. Emphasis is placed in particular on evaluating the pros and cons of alternative policy options, with an eye to developing appropriate strategies for action. The ambition is to play a meaningful role in the public arena. The intended audience is a wide range of engaged citizens and policy elites.

Some may see a resemblance of the first two possibilities to the distinction between explanation and understanding that has long bedeviled discussions of IR theory, particularly in Britain and the United States (Brown 2006). The distinction has been best articulated perhaps by Martin Hollis, a philosopher, and Steve Smith, an IR scholar, in their classic *Explaining and Understanding International Relations* (Hollis and Smith 1990). But the similarity to Comprehension and Critique is superficial at best. What Hollis and Smith had in mind were narrow modes of social inquiry – whether theories of IR should be "top down" (from system to unit) or "bottom up" (from unit to system) – not the underlying purpose of a broad field of study. Comprehension and Critique are meant to convey much more than merely the direction of causation in analytical models.

We have already encountered elements of each of the three Cs in Chapters 1 and 2. None is particularly novel. Nor are the three possible purposes necessarily mutually exclusive. As archetypes, their differences may be emphasized for purposes of contrast and comparison. In practice, however, there may well be considerable overlap among them. Indeed, the broader a field's tolerance for diversity, the more likely it is that we will see signs of two or even all three goals at work, even in the work of individual scholars. The practical question is not strictly either/or. Rather, it is a matter of *balance*. For a field like IPE, what is the best mix of the three and how can that mix be encouraged?

IPE TODAY

In IPE today across much of the globe, only two of the three possibilities are much in evidence. They are the first two – Comprehension and Critique. The pattern is clearly evident in most regions where the field has become established. As I have written elsewhere (Cohen 2019), that includes not just the Anglosphere (the English-speaking world) but also most of Continental Europe. Comprehension tends to be the main ambition of more orthodox perspectives, while Critique is at the heart of most heterodox approaches. Though in many ways diametric opposites, both Comprehension and Critique may be described as "academic" in the sense that each, in its own way, exalts the purity of theory and research. By contrast, as suggested in Chapter 1, relatively little effort in these regions is put into making a contribution to applied policy debate. The pattern tilts sharply away from proactive policy engagement and the messy world of politics. The overall mix is decidedly skewed.

The Mix

In the mix, the orthodox/heterodox divide is central. Even as the two sides of the divide are joined in their general disinterest in Counsel as a motivation, they tend to be sharply at odds over what should be emphasized in its place.

On the orthodox side, a focus on Comprehension as purpose is clearly implied by the priority given to strict objectivity and empiricism in research. Indeed, the tilt may be regarded as a natural corollary of hypothetico-deductivism. We know that among specialists who work in the American style, the aspiration, above all, is to uncover the fine details of how things work. For orthodox theorists, therefore, the triumph of Open Economy Politics (OEP) – an objective analytical approach backed by hard science methodology – is seen as a mark of genuine intellectual progress. David Lake proudly considers this a maturing of what he calls the "interdiscipline" of IPE (Lake 2006). In his words: "This young field is rapidly maturing. From a range of early perspectives ... IPE is now centered on, if you will, a hegemonic approach" (Lake 2006: 757, 772). In effect – to appropriate the language of Thomas Kuhn (1962) – a "paradigm shift" has occurred leading to a new era of "normal science." Again in Lake's words: "By the mid-1990s, OEP had dramatically reshaped the study of IPE in the United States and stimulated an ongoing period of Kuhnian normalcy" (Lake 2011: 47). Normal science means that researchers can concentrate mainly on micro- or mid-level theory, formulating and testing new conjectures about narrow causal relationships. The broader structures of global relations can be ignored or simply assumed as given. No deep disruption is needed.

On the heterodox side, meanwhile, it is much more about Critique: challenging, not accepting, the status quo. Broader global structures cannot just be shoved into the background. Rather, they must be problematized, their flaws and anomalies exposed, in the hope that inherited attitudes and practices can be radically transformed. The idea that IPE has matured into a normal science is rejected as a recipe for complacency or, worse, a defense of vested interests. To limit scholarship to dry scientific method is to neglect all that is wrong with the world. If the aim is to undermine the inertia that sustains the status quo, attention must be aroused. Disruption is a moral imperative. That too may be regarded as a natural corollary.

Missing from all this, by contrast, is much of a commitment – if any – to Counsel. Neither orthodoxy's normal science nor heterodoxy's appetite for opposition leave much room for applied policy analysis. Instead, disinterest in the public sphere is pervasive. Direct links between scholars and practitioners are scarce, and remarkably few members of IPE's invisible college show much eagerness to engage proactively with the policy process. Why the lack of interest? For some members of the invisible college, the messiness of policy debate threatens the purity of serious research. For others, the fear is that policy advice, however well designed, may simply be ignored by busy practitioners – an exercise in futility. Either way, the public arena is largely avoided. Most specialists prefer to remain at home in the ivory tower, even in places where policy-oriented research is formally promoted.

An apt case in point is provided by Britain's Research Excellence Framework (REF), a six-yearly exercise that determines how public research money is to be divided among UK departments and campuses. Programs are ranked based on a variety of criteria including policy engagement. In principle, as much as one-quarter of each program's score is based on "impact," meaning the ability to show that academic research can have a measurable effect on the behavior of non-academic stakeholders. In practice, though, as one London-based colleague wrote to me, the role of "impact" most often tends to be submerged. Everything, he declared ruefully, seems to "boil down to three things: publications, publications, publications."

There are exceptions, of course – researchers who really do make a commitment to Counsel. Some differences are a product of variations in local tradition. By and large, a distaste for public engagement is strongest in the United States (US), where the positivist norms of conventional social science tend to prevail. Across the border in Canada, by contrast, as well as in Australia and some European nations, a fair number of scholars have chosen to become actively involved in the policy process on an individual basis or through networks of formal advisory groups. And involvement is even more extensive in Latin America, where a tradition of state-centrism is of long standing. Latin Americans, going back to colonial times, typically expect the state to take a leading role in the management of economic affairs. Scholarship, therefore, more often than not has a public purpose. The aim is to bring insight to the problems facing governments and, where possible, to offer policy guidance (Cohen 2019: 111).

Other exceptions include scholars based in research organizations, who are more likely to see a role for themselves in the public arena than is typical of their university counterparts. No one doubts the influential role of think tanks like the Peterson Institute for International Economics in the US or the Royal Institute of International Affairs, commonly known as Chatham House, in Britain. Additionally, a scattering of instructional programs have now begun to emerge aiming to encourage more policy-relevant research by students of international relations (IR) or IPE. Among the most prominent is the well-funded Bridging the Gap Project at American University in Washington, DC. Bridging the Gap offers a variety of workshops and other initiatives designed to help make political and political-economy studies more accessible to non-academics. Likewise, in the rapidly expanding universe of social media, opportunities have increased for academics to disseminate their research and opine on policy issues. In the US, for instance, there is *The Monkey Cage*, a popular blog published by *The Washington Post* to connect political scientists with political conversation. A number of IPE specialists have made use of *The Monkey Cage* to get their views out. Other lively online venues are also available, such as *The Conversation* and *Project-Syndicate*. I myself have contributed to both. And, of course, there are platforms like Facebook or Twitter, which are open to all.

Overall, therefore, the invisible college is not without activist scholars – determined souls who feel driven to contribute to contemporary public debate. In the US apt examples include both political scientists like Dan Drezner and Kevin Gallagher and economists such as Dani Rodrik and Richard Feinberg. Elsewhere, we find the likes of Walden Bello in the Philippines, Jennifer Clapp in Canada, Diana Tussie in Argentina, and Robert Wade in Britain. Nor do the efforts of researchers like these go unremarked by others in IPE. For over a decade, Drezner has sponsored an annual award for best writing on political economy, nicknamed the Albie in honor of Albert Hirschman. And at the International Studies Association, the IPE section every year gives out an Outstanding Activist Scholar Award. The most recent recipients have included Heikki Patomäki (a Finn), Galia Golan (an Israeli), and Jackie Smith (an American). But high-flyers like these are relatively rare birds, still a distinct minority. Most of the species in our crowded field seem content to leave the challenge of practical policy analysis to others. For IPE overall, the mix remains decidedly skewed in favor of more "academic" pursuits.

Some Evidence

Nothing of this should come as much of a surprise to anyone familiar with the field. Most IPE specialists are aware of the dichotomy between orthodox and heterodox perspectives; and even if they rarely explore the differences between the two in any systematic fashion, they know – or think they know – enough about the other side to sense the contrasts of purpose. Orthodox theorists understand the compulsion of heterodoxy to seek a better world, even if they reject the moralizing that often goes with it. Heterodox theorists, conversely, can respect the demanding standards of orthodoxy even if they reject its style as an abdication of responsibility. The contrast is captured in an amusing image suggested by one recent source, which describes mainstream IPE as "the governing majority [whereas] critical IPE [is] the extra-parliamentary opposition" (Kranke 2014: 898).

Meanwhile, both sides seem to agree on an aversion for applied policy analysis, tilting the mix away from the public arena. In a systematic review of available data on journal articles and books in IPE, Jason Sharman and Catherine Weaver, two prominent researchers, found little evidence of policy engagement among their colleagues. In their words: "interest in policy relevant scholarship and outreach is not evident when we examine all of the data from published sources. There is very little work being published anywhere that either employs policy analysis as a method or makes explicit policy recommendations" (Sharman and Weaver 2013: 1093).

Additional evidence for this skewed pattern is not hard to find. As part of my preparation for this book, I undertook an informal opinion survey of friends and colleagues across the globe who are actively involved in IPE. More than four dozen scholars, scattered throughout the Anglosphere and Continental Europe, kindly consented to provide me with answers to a series of questions about the state of the field and where it might be going. Among my queries was one addressing the purpose of IPE. Strikingly, only a handful of colleagues bothered to respond to that particular question, suggesting that most had not ever thought much about the field's underlying goals. Those who did respond clearly confirmed the skewed mix I have described. On the one hand, preferences correlated closely with the orthodox/heterodox divide. Typical of views from the orthodox side was a noted American scholar who argued that "'basic' research – i.e., research for its own sake" should be "a fine primary objective for the field." Typical of voices from the heterodox side was a British researcher for whom the purpose of IPE is "to illuminate the inequalities and exploitative dynamics of the contemporary world." On the other hand, little was said on either side of the divide about the possibility of Counsel. Just one respondent suggested, in passing, that the field might "also contribute to policy and the public square." Otherwise, silence.

As a further part of my preparation for this book, I undertook four somewhat more formal surveys of relevant IPE publications that have appeared in various parts of the world. Here too the mix was repeatedly confirmed. The overwhelming favorites in the publications surveyed were again either Comprehension or Critique, depending on which side of the orthodox/heterodox divide authors or editors located themselves. Nowhere was a priority for Counsel entertained seriously.

In brief, the four surveys were:

1. An "Anglophone" survey. Already mentioned in Chapter 1, this survey systematically reviewed a representative sample of some three dozen textbooks or edited volumes of materials intended *inter alia* for use in IPE courses in the United States or elsewhere in the English-speaking world. The full list of sources can be found in Appendix B.
2. A "Left-Out" survey. Supplementing the Anglophone survey, this survey reviewed an additional sample of work in the English language by heterodox scholars, including especially Marxist and critical theorists who are often under-represented in more mainstream publications. The label for the survey is a kind of inside joke alluding to a commentary on my earlier *International Political Economy: An Intellectual History* (Cohen 2008) by the esteemed critical scholar Craig Murphy (2011). Murphy rightly took me to task for excluding from my discussion more radical IPE scholarship, which he wryly defined as "the 'Left-Out': scholars politically on the left" (Murphy 2011: 161). The full list of sources for this survey can be found in Appendix C.
3. A "European" survey. This survey covered a selection of material published in Britain or on the European continent. The full list of sources can be found in Appendix D.
4. A "Latin American" survey. This survey covered a representative sample of works by Latin American scholars (including some in the Spanish language). The full list of sources can be found in Appendix E.

The Anglophone survey is particularly persuasive since the range of perspectives represented in the sample was very wide, encompassing a variety of both orthodox and heterodox approaches. When it came to the subject of policy engagement, there was a remarkably uniform disregard for Counsel as a goal – almost a conspiracy of silence. While most of the sources had a good deal to say about what they see as the purpose of the field, little could be found that would seem intended to prepare students for a role in the public arena. The idea that a core purpose of IPE might be to offer practical policy advice was rarely mentioned, let alone advocated.

Instead, the emphasis was largely tilted toward either Comprehension or Critique. Most of the works in the sample used words like "understanding" or "explanation" (which is of course understandable since most of these publications were instructional, meant mainly for classroom use). IPE's purpose was "to explain," "to answer questions," "to elaborate," or "to draw connections." The main difference was over the motivations involved. For sources of a more orthodox persuasion, the purpose of IPE was understanding for its own sake – Comprehension *tout court*. No more needed to be said. But for sources of a more heterodox persuasion, much more needed to be said in order to make clear what wrongs must be made right. The following were typical:

> [The purpose of IPE] is to draw the connections among the structures of the economic domain, the (politicized) interests of the social groups and actors who participate in this structure (the structure-agent question), and the patterns of political conflict and change that take place within a particular set of domestic and international institutions. (Stubbs and Underhill 2006: 6)
> The purpose of the field [is] to expand voices and views of rising actors from the global south in the issue areas of finance, trade, and governance. (Mahrenbach and Shaw 2019: 1)
> [The purpose of IPE] is to comprehend how the struggle for power and wealth bring about development and conflict in the intersections between international–domestic, state–market, regional and global, formal and informal realities of development. (Vivares 2020: 1)

The China Exception

From this mix of preferences, however, there is one especially dramatic departure – China, the contemporary era's newest economic superstar. Paralleling that giant country's striking economic rise, Chinese interest in IPE has grown by leaps and bounds, particularly since the 1990s. Swiftly, the nation long known as the Middle Kingdom has become home to one of the invisible college's larger cohorts of specialists. In not much more than a generation, Chinese IPE scholarship has moved from rigid Marxist dogmas to a far more open and rapidly evolving field of study. Research is flourishing and momentum seems to be building to create a genuinely indigenous version of IPE – a school with, as the saying goes, "Chinese characteristics" – though the jury is still out on whether the effort will succeed (Cohen 2019).

Perhaps most notable about the field of IPE in China is a nearly universal emphasis on the centrality of the state. Not even in Latin America, with its colonial heritage, do we see such a single-minded focus on the role of government. Chinese scholars seem to have no interest in throwing off the "shackles of methodological nationalism." In the words of a recent commentary (Zhu and Pearson 2013: 1216), the Chinese literature "reflexively favours a strong role for the state ... and contains a normative presumption that the state is playing, and should continue to play, an important role." Constraints and opportunities for state behavior are explored at length. But the state itself, as a political institution, is rarely subjected to critical analysis. Most scholars simply take for granted that the sovereign nation is the key unit of interest. Implicitly, in line with Chinese historical tradition, governments are expected to act in the best interests of their citizens.

In turn, there appears to be little disagreement about the purpose of IPE research in China. It is normative: to offer advice to the state – specifically, the Chinese state – or to provide a form of justification for existing state policies (Wang and Hu 2017). The contrast with views to be found elsewhere, in societies where dissent is tolerated or even encouraged, is unmistakable. The vast majority of Chinese scholarship is unabashedly Sino-centric, driven by a widely shared nationalist mindset. China is seen as emerging from centuries of decay and humiliation, still seeking to determine its proper place in the world. Scholars see it as their role to help address problems facing the Middle Kingdom at a critical juncture of history. Hence research tends overwhelmingly to be policy driven. The aim is not to pursue positivist explanations or to build theory (Comprehension); nor, certainly, is it to find fault with the authoritarian rule of the Chinese Communist Party (Critique). Rather, the purpose is to be "useful" – to help China rise smoothly and smartly (Counsel). Most work follows a standard two-step format that has been labeled the "challenge-response" mode (Wang 2006: 364). First a challenge facing China's government is described; then policy recommendations (responses) are offered. Little effort goes into developing a theoretical component to link the two steps. The style is pragmatic, and the task is considered to be practical not conceptual. The aim, simply, is to serve the nation. If asked, Chinese scholars would undoubtedly say that they are merely being patriotic. For outsiders, the word "toadyism" might come to mind. There is little room for a genuinely critical tradition in a dictatorial political regime.

What explains the dominance of Sino-centric policy research in China? As I have suggested elsewhere (Cohen 2019), at least four key factors appear to be involved, which may be conceived in terms of a quartet of concentric circles. First, originating in the outermost circle, is the influence of the earliest translations of Western scholarship that made their way into Chinese universities and textbooks. For Robert Gilpin, Robert Keohane, and others of their pioneering generation, all trained in the political science sub-specialty of IR, it seemed only natural to make state policymaking their main concern. Reading the US classics, Chinese scholars were more or less conditioned to think the same way. Given IPE's late start in China, reliance on conceptual frameworks already developed elsewhere was quite understandable. One influential recent study (Pang and Wang 2013: 1205) concludes: "The strong socializing effect of Western IPE scholarship on China ... is perhaps natural given the short history of IPE in China." And this socializing effect has only been reinforced by the increasing numbers of Chinese youth returning to the Middle Kingdom after a period of study in the West.

Second, closer to home, is the influence of a parallel intellectual perspective that originated not in the West but in China's own East Asian neighborhood. That is the idea of the "developmental state," first popularized in the region by the phenomenal recovery of the Japanese economy following the destruction of World War II. Japan seemed to offer a distinctive model of economic management that put a proactive government at the center of the development process, harnessing private market forces to promote economic growth and other public policy goals. The model was soon adopted by other states in the region and, ultimately, by China itself. Chinese scholars could not help but be impressed by its relevance to their own nation's conditions and needs. Over time the model's theoretical underpinnings have been adapted to China's unique circumstances, gradually moving toward a more home-grown version of IPE.

Third, within China, is the influence of a long-standing cultural tradition, going back to Confucian times, that intellectual activity should not be divorced from public service. The notion of an academic ivory tower – of disinterested "objective" analysis – has little place in the history of the Middle Kingdom. Study was not valued for its own sake. Rather, academics were to be "scholar-officials," fully involved in affairs of state. The desire to be "useful" is built into the society's DNA, passed on from generation to generation for more than two millennia. The best way to honor one's family was to use one's studies to engage in public service. In such a milieu, there is nothing at all alien about falling into a "challenge-response" mode of scholarship.

Finally, within the Chinese academy, there is the influence of practical institutional structure. Virtually all universities and research centers in the Middle Kingdom are state institutions, extensions of the government and ruling party. Universities are run or controlled by the Ministry of Education; most research institutions are attached, directly or indirectly, to different ministries or provincial governments. This means that scholars are, in effect, state employees – not exactly bureaucrats, but certainly understood as public servants. Though there is no tradition of researchers taking temporary positions in government – as there is, for example, in the US – there is an expectation that they will produce useful advice to policymakers. All those aspiring to an academic career know that it is their role to contribute to broader policy discussions. Even if they were to prefer otherwise, they would feel impelled to put the state at the center of their research. Their careers depend on it.

To date, the Chinese focus on practical policy research has had little impact on the mix of preferences that generally prevails among IPE specialists elsewhere. That could change, of course, as others in the invisible college become more acquainted with what Chinese scholars are doing. The effort to learn more about the development of the field in China has begun (Chin et al. 2013). Shorn of its slavish fidelity to an authoritarian state, the Chinese understanding of purpose, with its emphasis on public service, could in time possibly gain more popularity. But for now it remains exceptional outside the borders of the Middle Kingdom.

JUDGING THE MIX

Strikingly, the mix of preferences that we find in IPE today is rarely, if ever, questioned. The field's purpose has not been much diagnosed systematically. Like Topsy, a character in the nineteenth-century anti-slavery novel *Uncle Tom's Cabin*, modern IPE just "growed." But after decades of drift, a more considered judgment of the prevailing pattern would by now seem to be called for. Why settle meekly for long-unaddressed assumptions? Below the surface, troubles are brewing, like a cancer.

In fact, I submit, two related pathologies threaten the field. One stems from the combative interaction between the two sides of the orthodox/ heterodox divide – a relationship that might best be described as one of *mutual animus*. The other entails the skewed interaction between the more "academic" preferences of both orthodox and heterodox scholarship, on the one hand, and applied policy research on the other – a relationship best characterized as one of *unilateral disdain*. Both pathologies stem from the careless manner in which the issue of purpose has been ignored over the years. In fact, at a very basic level, the two are both serious threats to the discipline's continued vigor. Without proper treatment, the cancer could spread.

Mutual Animus

At present, the mix of purposes in IPE that is evident across much of the globe is heavily skewed in favor of either Comprehension or Critique. Overall, though, neither goal is dominant, and between them the relationship has grown ever more contentious over time, like a failing marriage. Constant bickering can hardly be regarded as a sign of good marital health. Rather, it would seem to be best understood as a pathology in dire need of a cure. Some kind of prescription seems imperative.

A case can be made, of course, for doing nothing at all. Despite their mutual animus, the prevailing duopoly has seemingly served the field well until now. So why try to change it? As the old saying goes, "if it ain't broke, don't fix it." Call it the Open Door syndrome. From the modern field's modest beginning over a half-century ago, an open door meant that anyone with an interest in the politics of the world economy could freely enter. Admission was not limited to scholars with a single narrow purpose in mind, whether orthodox or heterodox. Variations of both themes were welcome. Hence goals could be taken for granted and growth of the field could proceed unimpeded. One wonders whether the field would have expanded so rapidly – or even expanded at all – had expectations been less tolerant. Arguably the successful (re)birth of IPE can be attributed, at least in part, to the Open Door syndrome. Moreover, now that the field is well established, the open door can be assumed to help avoid the stultifying dangers of a monoculture. The lack of a single dominant purpose means that there are no barriers to replenishment of

IPE's dense ecology. Dessication can be averted, allowing the field's fertility to be regularly refreshed.

However, an even stronger case can be made to the contrary. I contend that something is indeed broke and does need fixing. Call it the Stuck Door syndrome. When a door is stuck, unable to open or close properly, too much time tends to be wasted on thinking about the door itself rather than about what is on the other side. In IPE, what really matters is the interaction of economics and politics in international affairs. But because there is no agreed understanding about the field's ultimate goals, much energy is squandered on fractious and often distracting confrontations over perspective. Each faction in the invisible college finds it easier to judge other discourse coalitions in terms of its own preferences rather than by the norms of their counterparts. Effectively, for many, there is just one true faith; other creeds can simply be dismissed as non-conformist. Instead of judging the "normal science" of mainstream analysis on its technical merits, heterodox scholars too often just attack orthodoxy's reluctance to take a normative stand. Conversely, instead of engaging the social motivations of heterodox analyses on their own terms, orthodox scholars too often just brush aside moral or ethical considerations as insufficiently "objective." Meanwhile, the door remains stuck.

The problem of the stuck door is aptly illustrated by orthodoxy's treatment of the pioneering work of Robert Cox, who remains a lasting influence in places like Britain and Canada. For many heterodox scholars, Cox's notion of world orders remains a prime inspiration. Yet if acknowledged at all by more mainstream theorists, his work is received coolly, occasionally even with contempt, mainly because it is so infuriatingly at variance with the expectations of conventional social science. As Cox himself once ruefully conceded, "an interpretive, hermeneutic, historicist mode of knowledge lends itself to the epithet 'unscientific'" (Cox 1996: 29). Because of his propensity to mix positivist observation and moral judgments, many mainstream theorists have said that they find it difficult to assess the fundamental soundness of his reasoning. So rather than engage his work directly, they have found it easier simply to denounce or ignore him. Much the same treatment is also accorded to the legacy of Susan Strange despite her pivotal role in getting the field started half a century ago.

Conversely, heterodox scholars often spend more time attacking orthodoxy's broad principles than they do considering the substance of its analytical results. Here too we see a stuck door. Critics focus in particular on orthodoxy's emphasis on positivism. Pure objectivity in the social sciences, they argue, is impossible. Human beings are just not built that way. So why not join heterodoxy and come clean about unavoidable implicit biases? Cox's notorious dictum – "Theory is always *for* someone and *for* some purpose" (Cox 1981: 128) – is invoked repeatedly. As a trio of critical theorists wrote recently, "from a normative standpoint mainstream approaches can be considered to be ... not 'emancipatory' because they take basic socioeconomic and political structures as neutral categories, given and immutable ... The point of any theory is not simply to understand ... but also to uncover the ways in which purportedly objective analyses reflect the interests of those in positions of privilege and power" (Cafruny et al. 2016: 1–2).

In the eyes of heterodox theorists, to take the contemporary capitalist system as a given is, in effect, to make oneself complicit in all its evils. Orthodoxy has to be discredited from the start. As one recent commentary put it, radical researchers "see societal emancipation from capitalism as impossible without intellectual emancipation from mainstream approaches" (Kranke 2014: 899), thus excusing them from any obligation to take orthodoxy seriously. On their side too, heterodox scholars can simply denounce or ignore their opposites.

In short, neither side seems willing to look at things through the eyes of the other. The battle lines are clearly drawn. The danger is that over time the tension could prove tragic for the field as a whole. I have suggested that a certain degree of diversity can be a good thing – a strength as well as a weakness. But there can also be too much of a good thing if powerful centrifugal forces are let loose to rip the field asunder. The longer the mutual animus persists unabated, the more likely it is that irreversible rupture could follow. Ultimately the IPE amoeba could subdivide in much the same manner as did the ancestral disciplines of economics and political science in the nineteenth century, leaving a new dialogue of the deaf in their wake – a new Great Wall of silence. There is good reason why balkanization of the field is on the minds of many in the invisible college. Many of us can still recall what happened in the real-world Balkans of the 1990s when the old Yugoslavia dissolved in chaos. It would be a shame to see something similar happen to our field of study. Is IPE too destined to be wiped off the map and relegated to the history books?

Unilateral Disdain

For all their mutual animus, though, orthodoxy and heterodoxy do appear to share at least one prejudice in common – a unilateral disdain for policy engagement. The bias manifests itself in two ways. First is an evident reluctance to engage directly in applied policy analysis. Relatively little of what is published by IPE scholars is intended explicitly to offer practical advice on major issues of the day. And second is a failure to communicate effectively to policymakers even when advice is indeed the purpose. To be blunt, few academics seem to know how to write for an audience of non-academics. In the words of one practitioner: "Academics are lousy at marketing their policy-relevant research" (Radelet 2020: 102).

IPE is not alone in this respect, of course. Other specialties are also frequently guilty of the same sort of failing. Consider this recent lament from two prominent historians about their own academic discipline (Brands and Gavin 2018):

> [A]s the historical discipline ... became more professionalized, especially after World War II, it also became more specialized and inward-looking. Historical scholarship focused on increasingly arcane subjects; a fascination with innovative methodologies overtook an emphasis on clear, intelligible prose. Academic historians began writing largely for themselves.

Substitute "IPE" for "history" and the same point applies. Sadly, in our field, too, most academics have come to write largely for themselves. That is to be regretted. Arguably, there is much work in IPE, with its integration of both economic and political considerations, that could potentially be of use in the public arena, even if Counsel is not the work's ostensible aim. But what government official has the patience – or expertise – to plow through the coded language, elaborate hypotheses, and esoteric methodologies that characterize a typical journal article? Way back at the beginning of my professional career, when I was hired as a research economist at the Federal Reserve Bank of New York, I was told, in no uncertain terms, to use the simplest language possible in reporting my analyses to my superiors – and, above all, to never submit anything longer than nine pages. Anything more elaborate or with a page count greater than a single digit was bound to be set aside and never read. More recently, the theme was reiterated by a former high-level government official, who noted that "Neither policymakers nor their staff have time to wade through forty-page papers that cover literature reviews, methodological approaches, data issues, and results. They just aren't going to do it" (Radelet 2020: 102). Regrettably, among policy elites, neglect tends to be the fate of most of what appears in the IPE literature today. Indeed, researchers often seem to make it a point of pride to make their work as unreadable as possible. Unintelligibility, it would appear, is equated with advanced insight.

What drives this attitude? For most scholars in the field, unilateral disdain seems to come naturally. The risks of public engagement, it is feared, outweigh any benefits. Too often, policy analysis degenerates into little more than intellectual cover for professional biases of one kind or another. Too often as well, funding sources manage to tilt the balance by underwriting work that they know can be counted upon to offer support for their own point of view. As one veteran colleague put it to me privately: "Public engagement [becomes] conflated with sponsored research. Money talks." In some more authoritarian nations, there are also risks of a more personal nature. Particularly vocal scholars may be placed on an "enemies list" or possibly even imprisoned or exiled, as were many in Latin America during the era of military dictatorships in the 1970s and 1980s (Cohen 2019: 106–7).

Ultimately, the issue comes down to where it is thought IPE's conversations should properly be situated. Should discussion be confined mainly to the ivory tower – to strictly "academic" debates – to preserve the purity of scholarly research? Or, rather, might more effort be directed to public discourse, in hopes of making a useful practical contribution? Are we better off limiting ourselves to rigorously testing hypotheses and/or uncovering deep faults? Or should IPE move toward more proactive policy-oriented research – something like the Chinese model without the slavish political loyalty? Seemingly without much serious consideration, the field has drifted into a skew that largely disfavors participation in the public square. The battle line is drawn clearly here as well.

Not everyone in IPE concurs with this prejudice. Below the surface, much discontent with the pattern can be detected. That was definitely evident in the informal opinion survey that I undertook when preparing for this book. Answers in my sample appeared to show little interest in Counsel as a goal when queried specifically about the purpose of IPE. But in response to other questions, the issue kept bubbling up. One European colleague expressed frustration with the fact that "so little IPE work is read by policy-makers, think tankers, journalists and their assistants ... This is very disappointing because our field has so much to

Table 3.1   *IPE articles in four major journals, 2014–19*

	International Organization	Review of International Political Economy
IPE articles (total)	35	198
Comprehension (% of total)	91.4	84.3
Criticism (% of total)	0	5.1
Counsel (% of total)	8.6	9.6
	Foreign Affairs	International Affairs
IPE articles (% of totals)	15.0	14.4

say." Declared another expert: "We need more impassioned responses to the issues of the day." A good number agreed that the lack of systematic public engagement is a serious failing. But however deep the dissent may run, it has not had much influence on the way the field functions in actual practice.

To illustrate, I scanned all the articles published in the five years from 2015 to 2019 in two leading IPE journals, *International Organization* (*IO*) and the *Review of International Political Economy* (*RIPE*). Both publications are consistently ranked among the most highly regarded journals in the field (Seabrooke and Young 2017: 297). *IO*, a broad IR journal, is a favored venue for IPE research in the orthodox American style, while *RIPE* is more popular with heterodox scholars. Articles were classified according to the purpose that seemed most to animate them: Comprehension, Critique, or Counsel. As expected, papers that were devoted primarily to Comprehension or Critique dominated. The share of more policy-oriented work in the total of IPE pieces in either publication was in the single digits, just 8.6 percent for *IO* and 9.6 percent for *RIPE* – overall, a tiny handful. The full results are reported in the upper panel of Table 3.1.

Of course, neither *IO* nor *RIPE* can be considered a policy journal. Both are research publications dedicated to disseminating new theoretical and empirical studies and are intended mainly for an audience of scholars and students, not policymakers. So, I also scanned for the same period (2015–19) two leading journals that do aim more for an audience of policy elites – *Foreign Affairs*, published by the Council on Foreign Relations in New York, and *International Affairs*, the house journal of Britain's Chatham House. These two also are among the most highly regarded journals in IPE (Seabrooke and Young 2017: 297). If policy-oriented work does get done in the field, this is where we would expect to find much of it. Yet in both publications the share of IPE pieces in the total number of articles published was remarkably small, no more than 15 percent of the total in any one year – again, a tiny handful. The results are reported in the lower panel of Table 3.1.

Similar results come from a quartet of industrious scholars at the College of William and Mary – the same group that created and still manages the well-known Teaching, Research and International Policy (TRIP) Project. For almost two decades the TRIP Project has provided us with a series of valuable surveys of the broad discipline of IR (including IPE), based on both opinion polls and reviews of the most highly rated field journals. Most recently, the quartet organized a volume of invited essays by prominent American IR and IPE scholars, aimed precisely at the paucity of policy engagement in the literature. The title tells it all: *Bridging the Theory–Practice Divide in International Relations* (Maliniak et al. 2020). Included in the collection are almost a score of commissioned papers by scholars and practitioners on a range of topics in IR, including two that deal directly with the core issues of IPE – one on trade relations by Edward Mansfield and Jon Pevehouse (2020) and one on money and finance by Thomas Pepinsky and David Steinberg (2020). The findings of the two essays are strikingly similar. Among articles published in leading journals on either trade or finance, no more than 5 percent made explicit policy recommendations. The detachment from policy matters was unmistakable. IPE scholars, Pepinsky and Steinberg conclude sadly, are "unwilling to engage with policymakers' priorities" (Pepinsky and Steinberg 2020: 136).

Like the mutual animus between orthodoxy and heterodoxy, the overall prejudice against policy engagement should also be treated as a pathology in need of a cure. At the moment, neither side of the orthodox/heterodox divide does much to advance Counsel as an alternative to the more traditional "academic" pursuits of Comprehension or Critique. Indeed, both sides tend to display a distinct disinclination to sully themselves directly in the public arena. That skewed mix seems to have become a stable feature of our field. Over time, however, the bias against policy engagement could prove tragic if it leads outsiders to question why the field exists at all. What does IPE have to offer if all that its invisible college wants to do is play word games back in the ivory tower? Should it not also have something of practical value to offer the larger community? Should it not also have some grander purpose? Or are IPE specialists no more than futile "eggheads?"

Compare IPE today with the economics discipline, which has long managed to contribute usefully to public debate without any sacrifice of intellectual integrity. No one called John Maynard Keynes an egghead. Economics has no need to justify its existence as a distinct and respected field of study. But for how long will the same be said for IPE? For how long will the field be able to attract resources and talent if it continues to stand aloof from the struggles of everyday life? The longer the disdain for policy engagement persists, the greater is the risk that the field will come to be dismissed as marginal at best – little more than a campus sideshow, irrelevant and innocuous. IPE would then be lost. To save it, some kind of prescription seems imperative here as well.

RETHINKING THE MIX

Can the battle lines be redrawn? Better yet, can they be eliminated? My answer is: Yes, healing is indeed possible. Overcoming decades of drift is unlikely to be easy, of course. (If it were easy, it probably would have already happened.) But with determined effort, I submit, it can be done. It is not too late. Doctors tell us that most pathologies can be managed reasonably well, if not cured, when the diagnosis is right. What we need are proper prescriptions.

Mutual Animus

For the mutual animus that pervades the field, the proper prescription is to learn how to see through the other's eyes. It is unlikely that the other side is all wrong; nor is it likely that you are totally right. If fragmentation of the field is to be avoided, mutual animus must be replaced by mutual sympathy, maybe even mutual respect.

The lesson is well illuminated by an old story that I was told as a child. It is a tale about a sagacious rabbi in a small Eastern European Jewish community centuries ago who was called upon to referee a dispute between two neighbors. The first neighbor made his case, and the rabbi declared "You're right." The second neighbor then presented his case and again the rabbi declared "You're right." Pandemonium broke out as witnesses protested that, surely, they couldn't both be right, and the rabbi quietly declared yet again "You're right." In good Talmudic tradition, the story has many interpretations. But I am convinced that what the rabbi was really trying to do was to persuade the two neighbors to see through each other's eyes. Each was convinced of his own rightness. The rabbi wanted them to see that the other could also legitimately claim to have some right on his side. That is what we need in IPE as well: an Open Door, not a Stuck Door.

The key to opening the door lies in the structure of incentives that channel work in the field. That takes us back to the very practical issue of professional advancement, which like the CMB is always lurking behind the scenes. Scholars are no less interested in material success than other professionals. At the personal level rewards come in the form of faculty appointments, promotion, tenure, or salary. More broadly, the drive for achievement brings recognition, reputation, and prestige. The challenge for IPE is to restructure payoffs in a way that generates a significant increase of return for efforts to promote better understanding across the orthodox/heterodox divide. I will have more to say on this critical matter in Chapter 6.

Unilateral Disdain

For the pathology of unilateral disdain, the proper prescription would be to elevate Counsel as a goal for the field. No longer should policy engagement take a distant second place to Comprehension and Critique among IPE's purposes. If the field is to justify its existence, it must demonstrate that it really has something of value to offer the larger community – a serious contribution to discourse in the public arena. That does not mean supplanting Comprehension or Critique; there must always be a place for the many in the field whose work is without immediate policy application or who lack a taste for acrimonious public debate. But it does mean seeking to achieve a better overall balance among the three possible goals. More of the invisible college should be encouraged to climb down from the ivory tower and get their hands dirty.

How might that be done? Britain's REF makes a nod in the right direction by including "impact" among its criteria for distributing public research money. But the REF exercise evaluates the collective activity of whole departments, not individual scholars. What is needed is more effort to prioritize public engagement in as much of our work as possible. To begin, a greater emphasis could be placed on communicating effectively to policymakers. It may not be possible to make many journal articles more readable. Formal research must continue to meet high standards in terms of both theory and methods. But it might be possible to complement formal policy-relevant publications with parallel slimmed-down versions that are more readily accessible to non-specialists. That is not an unfamiliar strategy and can be accomplished either in print publications or via social media. Examples can be found in online venues like *The Monkey Cage* or *Project-Syndicate*. A fine recent example in print was provided by Henry Farrell and Abraham Newman, who illuminated some of the ways in which the networks of a globalized world economy can be "weaponized" by powerful states. In true scholarly fashion, they first published a formal research paper embodying their findings in a prominent IR journal, *International Security* (Farrell and Newman 2019); the article was also later reprinted it in an edited collection of commentaries by prominent specialists (Drezner et al. 2021). But, in addition, the pair also quickly followed with more popular versions in a widely read policy journal (Farrell and Newman 2020) and in a major newspaper (Newman 2019), reaching very different audiences. Regrettably, however, that is not a strategy that is employed by many in the IPE field.

Beyond that, it ought to be possible to put more emphasis on research design as well, in order to make results more directly useful to policy elites. In Chapter 1, for instance, I referred to IPE's problem with time – the tendency to be mostly backward-looking in nature. The logic is well articulated by Mary Tyrone, one of the characters in Eugene O'Neill's *Long Day's Journey into Night*, who declares that "The past is the present, isn't it? It's the future, too." William Faulkner had much the same thought in mind when he memorably lamented that in the Deep South of the US (the states that were on the losing side in America's Civil War), "The past is never dead. It's not even past." But as I suggested, that leaves us ill-prepared for the many "unknown unknowns" that might crop up in the future. Think earthquakes, volcanic eruptions, or perhaps even a novel coronavirus. For public officials, even the recent past is already ancient history. IPE, for them, would offer greater value if more studies were focused directly on days to come, using available planning techniques to assess the challenges and implications of alternative future scenarios. Here a prime example is provided by Miles Kahler, a respected US scholar, who in a recent paper systematically compared three alternative futures for global economic governance: fragmentation, stagnation, and transformation (Kahler 2018).

Here too, as with the pathology of mutual animus, the key lies in the structure of incentives that channel work in the field. Typically, the highest honors in IPE – as in most of the social sciences – go to those who hew most closely to the norms of purely "academic" scholarship. That means extensively researched articles or books that purport to push out the frontiers of knowledge in one way or another. It also means that the choice of topics is often of less importance than the novelty of the theory or the cleverness of the methodology. Here too the challenge for IPE is to restructure professional payoffs – in this instance, in a way that generates a significant increase of return for studies that are policy-relevant and clearly presented. I will have more to say in Chapter 6 on this critical matter as well.

CONCLUSION

The aim of this chapter has been to rethink the purpose of IPE as a field of study. The question of the field's goals has rarely been addressed formally. Upon reflection, however, it becomes clear that in practice the preferred motives are largely "academic," emphasizing positivist explanations and/or normative critiques rather than applied policy engagement. The health of the field is threatened by two dangerous pathologies, which I have labeled "mutual animus" and "unilateral disdain." Mutual animus pits orthodoxy against heterodoxy and could lead to irreversible fragmentation of the field. Unilateral disdain discourages contributions to public discourse and risks seeing the field condemned to irrelevance. In both cases prescriptions are possible. But all would take considerable determination to overcome allegiance to the status quo. We will come back to the all-important practicalities of implementation in the final chapter.

REFERENCES

Brands, Hal and Francis J. Gavin (2018), "The Historical Profession is Committing Slow-Motion Suicide," *War on the Rocks*, December 10. Retrieved from https://warontherocks.com/2018/12/the-historical-profession-is-committing -slow-motion-suicide

Brown, Chris (2006), "IR Theory in Britain – the New Black?" *Review of International Studies* 32:4, 677–87.

Cafruny, Alan W., Gonzalo Pozo Martin, and Leila Simona Talani (2016), "Introduction," in Alan W. Cafruny, Gonzalo Pozo Martin, and Leila Simona Talani, eds., *The Palgrave Handbook of Critical International Political Economy* (London: Palgrave Macmillan), 1–6.

Chin, Gregory, Margaret M. Pearson, and Wang Yong, eds. (2013), "International Political Economy in China: The Global Conversation," *Review of International Political Economy*, special issue, 20:6.

Cohen, Benjamin J. (2008), *International Political Economy: An Intellectual History* (Princeton, NJ: Princeton University Press).

Cohen, Benjamin J. (2019), *Advanced Introduction to International Political Economy*, 2nd edition (Cheltenham, UK and Northampton, MA, USA: Edward Elgar Publishing).

Cox, Robert W. (1981), "Social Forces, States, and World Orders: Beyond International Relations Theory," *Millennium* 10:2, 126–55.

Cox, Robert W. (1996), "Influences and Commitments," in Robert W. Cox and Timothy J. Sinclair, eds., *Approaches to World Order* (New York: Cambridge University Press), 19–38.

Drezner, Daniel W., Henry Farrell, and Abraham L. Newman, eds. (2021), *The Uses and Abuses of Weaponized Interdependence* (Washington, DC: Brookings Institution).

Farrell, Henry and Abraham L. Newman (2019), "Weaponized Interdependence: How Global Economic Networks Shape State Coercion," *International Security* 44:1, 42–79.

Farrell, Henry and Abraham L. Newman (2020), "Chained to Globalization: Why It's Too Late to Decouple," *Foreign Affairs* 99:1, 70–80.

Hollis, Martin and Steve Smith (1990), *Explaining and Understanding International Relations* (Oxford: Clarendon Press).

Kahler, Miles (2018), "Global Governance: Three Futures," *International Studies Review* 20:2, 239–46.

Kranke, Matthias (2014), "Which 'C' Are You Talking About? Critical Meets Cultural IPE," *Millennium*, 42:3, 897–907.

Kuhn, Thomas S. (1962), *The Structure of Scientific Revolutions* (Chicago: University of Chicago Press).

Lake, David A. (2006), "International Political Economy: A Maturing Interdiscipline," in Barry R. Weingast and Donald A. Wittman, eds., *Oxford Handbook of Political Economy* (New York: Oxford University Press), 757–77.

Lake, David A. (2011), "TRIPs across the Atlantic: Theory and Epistemology in IPE," in Nicola Phillips and Catherine E. Weaver, eds., *International Political Economy: Debating the Past, Present and Future* (London: Routledge), 45–52.

Mahrenbach, Laura C. and Timothy M. Shaw (2019), "Continuities and Change in IPE at the Start of the Twenty-first Century," in Timothy M. Shaw, Laura C. Mahrenbach, Renu Modi, and Xu Yi-chong, eds., *The Palgrave Handbook of Contemporary International Political Economy* (London: Palgrave Macmillan), 1–23.

Maliniak, Daniel, Susan Peterson, Ryan Powers, and Michael J. Tierney, eds. (2020), *Bridging the Theory–Practice Divide in International Relations* (Washington, DC: Georgetown University Press).

Mansfield, Edward D. and Jon. C. Pevehouse (2020), "Trade Policy and Trade Policy Research," in Daniel Maliniak, Susan Peterson, Ryan Powers, and Michael J. Tierney, eds., *Bridging the Theory–Practice Divide in International Relations* (Washington, DC: Georgetown University Press), 105–18.

Murphy, Craig N. (2011), "Do the Left-Out Matter?" in Nicola Phillips and Catherine E. Weaver, eds., *International Political Economy: Debating the Past, Present and Future* (London: Routledge), 160–8.

Newman, Abraham L. (2019), "US and China are Weaponising Global Trade Networks," *Financial Times*, September 1. Retrieved from https://www.ft .com/content/a8ab8cd2-c99c-11e9-af46-b09e8bfe60c0.

Pang, Zhongying and Hongying Wang (2013), "Debating International Institutions and Global Governance: The Missing Chinese IPE Contribution," *Review of International Political Economy*, 20:6, 1189–1214.

Pepinsky, Thomas B. and David A. Steinberg (2020), "Is International Relations Relevant for International Money and Finance?" in Daniel Maliniak, Susan Peterson, Ryan Powers, and Michael J. Tierney, eds., *Bridging the Theory–Practice Divide in International Relations* (Washington, DC: Georgetown University Press), 129–45.

Radelet, Steven (2020), "Making Academic Research on Foreign Aid More Policy Relevant," in Daniel Maliniak, Susan Peterson, Ryan Powers, and Michael J. Tierney, eds., *Bridging the Theory–Practice Divide in International Relations* (Washington, DC: Georgetown University Press), 97–103.

Reynolds, Philip (1987), "Of Politics and Paradigms," *Review of International Studies* 13, 61–7.

Seabrooke, Leonard and Kevin L. Young (2017), "The Networks and Niches of International Political Economy," *Review of International Political Economy* 24:2, 288–331.

Sharman, Jason C. and Catherine Weaver (2013), "*RIPE*, the American School and Diversity in Global IPE," *Review of International Political Economy* 20: 5, 1082–1100.

Stubbs, Richard and Geoffrey R.D. Underhill (2006), "Introduction: Conceptualizing the Changing Global Order," in Richard Stubbs and Geoffrey R.D. Underhill, eds., *Political Economy and the Changing Global Order*, 3rd edition (Toronto, Oxford, and New York: Oxford University Press), 3–23.

Vivares, Ernesto (2020), "Introduction," in Ernesto Vivares, ed., *The Routledge Handbook to Global Political Economy: Conversations and Inquiries* (New York and London: Routledge), 1–8.

Wang, Hongying and Xue Ying Hu (2017), "The New Great Leap Forward: Think Tanks with Chinese Characteristics," CIGI Paper 142 (Waterloo, Canada: Center for International Governance and Innovation).

Wang, Jun (2006), "The Research on China's Sovereignty Issue," in Wang Yizhou, ed., *IR Studies in China, 1995–2005* (Beijing: Peking University Press). [Original in Chinese]

Zhu, Tianbiao and Margaret Pearson (2013), "Globalization and the Role of the State: Reflections on Chinese International and Comparative Political Economy Scholarship," *Review of International Political Economy* 20:6, 1215–43.

4. Rethinking diversity

We come next to the How question: How should we study International Political Economy (IPE)? Since the first days of the (re-)emergence of modern IPE, the field has lacked any sort of common analytical core. Paradigms have proliferated. We have many research traditions to choose from, each offering a different path to inquiry. This colorful diversity, I have suggested, may be regarded as both a strength and a weakness. Arguably, a multiplicity of theoretical approaches enhances the richness of the field. But it can also lead to dissonance and discord, with specialists unable to agree even on first principles. We need to rethink what can or should be done about the field's diversity. The key, I would argue, lies in accepting that, like it or not, all that variety is here to stay. So why not make the best of it?

David Lake speaks for many when he calls for a "tolerance for pluralism" (Lake 2011: 51). But passive forbearance alone, I would argue, is insufficient. We need to go further, to be more proactive in confronting IPE's proliferation of analytical perspectives. We need to learn how to *benefit* from the full range of what the field has to offer – to fully *exploit* its richness – rather than go about denying or denouncing it. Our mantra should be: don't deplore diversity – instead, put it to good use.

THE PROBLEM

To begin, what is the problem? We must be clear. The problem is not diversity per se. Diversity itself is not a sin. Quite the opposite, niche proliferation is a natural state of affairs in every academic discipline, as I noted back in Chapter 1. The celebrated economist Robert Mundell, often referred to as the father of the euro, liked to joke that the optimum population of currencies in the world was an odd number less than three. That may well be true in the case of money, although there are also many who might beg to differ (Cohen 2004). But it would almost certainly not be true for a field of study such as IPE. That way, to repeat, lies aridity and desiccation. Competing paradigms are a sign of spirit and creativity.

In practical terms, diversity is simply a menu of options: different ways to think about how the world works. The fuller the menu, the more freedom we have in choosing how to frame analysis. The problem lies in what we do – or don't do – with that freedom. Diversity can be a blessing or a curse. The choice is ours.

Curse?

The potential disadvantages of diversity have already been touched upon in previous chapters. There are at least three ways that a multiplicity of theoretical approaches can prove to be a curse for a field of study like IPE.

First, it may simply be *confusing*. Paradigms come in all shapes and sizes, as we saw in Chapter 2, each with its own set of basic ideas and assumptions about how the world works. We in the field may all be members of the same invisible college. But with our diverse patterns of training and socialization, we tend to see things through distinctly different eyes. Theorists educated in the positivist style of political science in the United States (US) may be excused if they find it difficult to grasp the mysteries of critical theory or cultural IPE, with their specialized language and unfamiliar concepts. Likewise, scholars with a background in sociology or history often find work built on neoclassical economic models downright incomprehensible. Niche proliferation may be an entirely natural process in the academic world. But as the number of discourse coalitions grows, the risk of mutual misunderstanding rises exponentially.

Second, as misunderstanding grows, the risk of *conflict* increases as well. The Stuck Door syndrome rears its ugly head, as it so often does in IPE and the study of international relations (IR). Divergent discourse coalitions may crystalize into contentious factions, giving rise to rancor and rebuke. As indicated in the previous chapter, we already see much evidence of this process at work in the mutual animus that prevails between the two sides of the orthodox/heterodox divide in IPE. Further tensions are evident within each of the two broad categories – in pitched battles between liberals and realists or between neo-utilitarian and cognitive approaches on the orthodox side of the divide, or between variants of system-level theory or critical theory on the heterodox side. Established scholars hate it when paradigm wars break out. "I have relatively little patience for the Great Debates in IR and IPE," declares Lake. "I often wish that scholars would stop contemplating *how* to do research and simply get on with the business" (Lake 2011: 45; emphasis in the original). Eric Helleiner labels it "navel gazing" (Helleiner 2011a: 178). But like it or not, the risk is always there.

Third, conflict in turn may result in outright *fragmentation*, as suggested in the previous chapter. Balkanization could become irreparable. Debates between diverse schools of thought may begin politely enough, addressing legitimate questions of academic standards: What constitutes knowledge or what represents valid research? But ultimately discussion comes down to a matter of values – what may be seen as more or less vital. And because professional reputations are at stake, arguments often have an "unfortunate tendency," as Lake puts it, "to become highly personalized and vitriolic" (Lake 2011: 45). It is easy to understand, therefore, why in time polemics may take on the tone of religious warfare, with every faction stubbornly entrenched in its own set of beliefs. Subdivision or dissolution of a field of study can easily follow.

Blessing?

But that is only half the story. On the other hand, diversity may also be distinctly advantageous to a field of study like IPE. That is the Open Door syndrome. When the door is open rather than stuck, a multiplicity of theoretical perspectives allows subjects to be explored from many different angles, using a variety of frames. Many specialists boast of IPE's "depth and range of analytical enlightenment," as two British scholars put it (Green and Hay 2015: 334). IPE researchers, the pair adds, "should continue to assert the richness of our diverse and inter-disciplinary approaches." A menu of options is there for the taking. In effect, diversity can act as a sort of "force multiplier" to fill gaps or add insight to ongoing research and analysis.

Recall that simplification is at the core of any paradigm. Assumptions are made, explicitly or implicitly, about some aspects of reality in hopes of then being able to say something meaningful about other aspects of reality. Hence there is always a good chance that in any given model something important may be left out that could conceivably distort or qualify – or, alternatively, enhance or confirm – analytical results. Where such "omitted-variable bias" is known to exist, an appeal to another theoretical perspective might well serve to resolve the issue, adding power to an argument.

I have already alluded in Chapter 1 to the disadvantage of relying on a single theoretical perspective – a research strategy variously labeled "singularism" (Grieco 2019) or "monism" (Wullweber 2019). A major attraction of singularism is its seeming clarity. By choosing to limit all work to just one paradigm, it facilitates more parsimonious analysis. The number of possible causal variables is limited. Hence conclusions may be sharper and less contingent. But parsimony comes at a price – most importantly, the risk of omitted-variable bias. Key factors and relationships may be left out, leaving theoretical models seriously under-specified. Diversity makes it possible to compensate for the risk of omitted-variable bias by expanding the scope of research.

An apt illustration is Thomas Oatley's notion of the "reductionist gamble," previously mentioned in Chapter 2 (Oatley 2011). At issue for Oatley, writing a decade ago, was the methodological reductionism of the Open Economy Politics (OEP) paradigm, which as codified by Lake assumes a state-centric world in which causation runs overwhelmingly in just one direction – from inside the state outward. In effect, the approach takes a risky bet that there are no offsetting causal relations of any consequence flowing the other way, from outside the state inward. But Oatley convincingly showed, and much subsequent research has confirmed, that in many cases the reductionist gamble may indeed miss important "outside-in" influences – what he calls "macro processes." In his words: "The political choices that OEP strives to explain are typically a product of the interplay between domestic politics and macro processes. When OEP casually omits causally significant macro processes from empirical models, the models yield biased inferences" (Oatley 2011: 311). In short, reciprocal interactions between the domestic and international levels of analysis cannot be ignored. As indicated previously, more recent studies have quite self-consciously sought to follow Oatley's lead, integrating both levels of analysis to amplify the power of their arguments (Farrell and Newman 2016; Walter 2016; Widmaier 2016; Blyth and Matthijs 2017).

Another illustration was provided by the introduction of constructivism into IPE starting about three decades ago. Theoretical approaches that highlighted the role of personal beliefs and intersubjective understandings offer a way to fill in some of the blanks left by more traditional neo-utilitarian studies. And similarly, on the heterodox side of the divide, much the same can be said of the several proposed extensions of IPE described in Chapter 2, each of which has aimed to add a neglected dimension to prior frameworks of analysis. Just as the risk of mutual misunderstanding may grow with greater diversity, so too may opportunities for force multiplication.

PATHOLOGIES

Obviously, blessings are preferred to curses. But the downsides of diversity are real – the flip side of the coin, as it were – and cannot be just wished away. To sustain the good health of the field, they should not be allowed to fester. Two twin-like pathologies can be identified here, which may be called *inadvertent omission* and *overt opposition*. Regrettably, there is abundant evidence of both afflicting today's IPE.

Inadvertent Omission

On the one hand, there is the possibility that research based on one theoretical approach alone will simply *omit* any reference to possible insights that might be derived from other paradigms or perspectives. The cause of the omission may be quite inadvertent. More often than not, it is due to nothing more than an innocent lack of awareness of what other traditions might have to contribute – a kind of intellectual myopia. It is like an old joke about a tailor from New York, a simple man with few interests beyond his sewing, who manages to get an audience with the pope. When he returns home, excited friends ask what the Holy Father is like. The tailor replies: "He's a 40-regular."

Regrettably, as suggested in Chapter 1, many students of IPE tend to be like the tailor. Trained, typically, in just a single version of the field, they come to be safely segregated into separate silos. Insularity is initially promoted in the classroom and then subsequently reinforced by professional socialization. The natural incentive, of course, is to meet the standards of one's own cohort. But the regrettable result, in the words of one keen observer, tends to be a form of "alienated pluralism" – in bluntest terms, "sheer ignorance" (Young 2021). Much too often, scholars fail to appreciate the relevance of what might be discovered in other silos. The danger, accordingly, is that much of value may be foregone. In effect, alternative theoretical approaches are like foreign languages. If you never studied the language and you lack a good translator, you have no way of knowing what you are missing. You remain myopic.

The problem of inadvertent omission is widely recognized. As one friend lamented to me in private correspondence, "the different strands of IPE do not speak to each other ... they do not even read or reference each other." A former lead editor of the *Review of International Political Economy* (*RIPE*) echoes this: "We have allowed ourselves to become so entrenched in our imagined communities or defensive of our respective identities that we fail to utilise emerging comparative strengths and exchange ideas across the divide in a constructive or even competitive manner" (Weaver 2011: 146). Instead, silence reigns. Who knows what value is consequently lost?

Anyone familiar with the field could cite multiple examples. Just a few years ago, an instructive case was provided by none other than David Lake on the occasion of his well-earned election as president of the American Political Science Association (Lake 2018). His presidential address, entitled "International Legitimacy Lost? Rule and Resistance when America is First," set out to explore the causes and consequences of the seeming erosion of the US-led liberal international order after the 2016 election of Donald Trump. As befitted his political science audience, much of his discussion focused on domestic governance and international security. But in accord with his own background in IPE, room was provided as well for the interplay of economics and politics on a global scale. Overall, Lake's analysis was astute and full of insight, especially in his deft integration of material and cognitive considerations. But the approach was pure OEP – state-centric from the start and building outward from domestic interests to international bargaining. Not surprisingly, given the ahistorical character of the OEP paradigm, Lake struggled to get a firm grasp on the issue of systemic transformation and showed no interest in, or even awareness of, the rich tapestry of system-level theories available in IPE. That did not make his argument wrong, but his myopia did make his observations thinner.

Nor is Lake alone in that respect. Orthodox scholars in general tend to be much more often guilty of the sin of inadvertent omission than theorists of more heterodox persuasion. The explanation is straightforward. The American school, with all its variants, is widely seen as occupying a hegemonic position among the many factions in IPE's invisible college. The US stands out in surveys identifying the field's most influential scholars and programs (Cohen 2019: chapter 9). Moreover, the American school dominates in terms of sheer numbers and resources. Its adherents, therefore, take the designation "mainstream" to heart. Secure in their own way of seeing the world, they generally feel little need to explore other perspectives, which are thought of as little more than insignificant minor tributaries. Parochial would not be an unfair description of their attitude; maybe even patronizing. Most heterodox theorists, by contrast, believe they have no choice but to make themselves familiar with more orthodox thought if their own work is to be taken seriously. They have to know what they are up against. For them, the myopia of inadvertent omission is a luxury they can ill afford.

Overt Opposition

On the other hand, there is the possibility that other theoretical approaches may be not omitted but actively *rejected*. The curse of conflict takes over. That is the Stuck Door syndrome, where energy is wasted on needless confrontation. Alternative paradigms may be acknowledged, but as foes to be vanquished rather than as force multipliers to add value. They become foils, not allies. The posture is not innocence but animus. The danger is paradigm war.

Here too, anyone familiar with the field of IPE could cite multiple examples in the literature. In this case, however, relatively fewer instances are to be found among orthodox scholars. Why take the time to denounce rival approaches if they are so insignificant? In the words of a senior colleague at one of America's top universities, who confided to me privately, "there really is not much room for discussion ... There is simply not enough common language or enough common understanding ... Conversations across this barrier are essentially fruitless."

For more heterodox theorists, however, who define themselves directly by their opposition to mainstream thought, a more aggressive posture may seem to them essential to ensure differentiation and garner respect. Contrariness is in their genes (or at least in the roots of the word heterodoxy). The aim, often, seems to be not just to reject but to delegitimize the opposition. Illustrative is a memorable diatribe by Peter Burnham, a respected British academic, which was featured in *RIPE* during the journal's inaugural year a quarter of a century ago. Burnham's target was the mainstream version of IPE imported from the United States. Orthodox IPE, he wrote, is a "vulgar, fraudulent discipline [that] eschews a study of social relations, opting instead for a crude amalgam of neoclassical economics, pluralist domestic political science and realist international relations theory ... The Americans fail to grasp the complex organic set of social relations which is the global political economy" (Burnham 1994: 221). The intensity of animosity here was hard to miss.

To be sure, Burnham's diatribe was not without merit. It may be a bit unfair to label orthodox IPE – today codified in the OEP paradigm – as vulgar or fraudulent. But as I noted back in Chapter 1, the mainstream US approach does indeed rely heavily on old models borrowed from economics and political science, leaving it to this day vulnerable to

Burnham's kind of attack. A quarter of a century after Burnham's diatribe, many heterodox theorists still see the same fatal defects. Ernesto Vivares, for instance, an Argentinian who teaches in Ecuador, writes that OEP "is outdated, limited and rather insufficient ... showing severe constraints in its scholarship when it comes to comprehending unforeseen changes" (Vivares 2020: 10). Not all heterodox scholars would express themselves with quite so much vinegar as do Burnham and Vivares. But there is little doubt that most of them take pride in their own style of IPE and are prepared to fight to defend it.

AN ILLUSTRATION

An apt illustration of these twin pathologies is provided by the voluminous literature that followed the global financial crisis (GFC) of 2008 – prior to the recent coronavirus pandemic, the worst shock to the world economy in living memory. Theorists have persistently struggled to explain what went wrong. In November 2008, during a visit to the London School of Economics, Queen Elizabeth II innocently asked: "If these things were so large, how come everyone missed them?" The question was hardly unreasonable. In post mortem after post mortem, IPE scholars have sought to provide a satisfactory answer. Along the way we see abundant evidence of both inadvertent omission and overt opposition.

Orthodoxy

For many observers, including myself (Cohen 2009, 2017), the answer to the Queen's question lay in the myopia of mainstream scholarship. That includes the work of conventional economists as well as the more orthodox side of IPE where, as often noted, broader structures are rarely problematized. Few researchers working in the American style in the years before 2008 betrayed much suspicion that we might be skating on increasingly thin ice. Their record in this respect was dismal, not to say embarrassing. For the most part, the possibility of a serious systemic crash was simply ignored – a prime example of inadvertent omission.

Evidence of the myopia is easy to find. A quick scan of articles published in the decade prior to the GFC in five top US journals (*International Organization, International Studies Quarterly, World Politics, American Political Science Review*, and *American Journal of Political Science*) reveals remarkably few studies that even broached the subject of financial crisis – fewer than a dozen in all. Moreover, of this handful almost all were essentially backward-looking, limiting themselves mainly to explaining policy responses to banking or currency failures in the past.

Some articles concentrated on distributional issues and the role of key interest groups. One prominent US scholar, for example, undertook a detailed analysis of Congressional roll calls on financial rescues organized for Mexico and several East Asian nations in the 1990s (Broz 2005). He found strong evidence of the impact of private-sector interests on legislative voting patterns. Another researcher documented the salience of varying constituency coalitions in accounting for differences in adjustment policies adopted by countries like Indonesia and Malaysia during the Asian emergency of 1997–8 (Pepinsky 2008). And still others focused on the part played by domestic institutions – political regime type, degrees of central-bank independence, or variations in executive accountability – in shaping governmental reactions to financial crisis (Hicken et al. 2005; Rosas 2006; Keefer 2007). In most cases the research was thorough and insightful. None could be accused of failing to meet a high standard of scholarship; all were astute about the politics involved. Yet, collectively, there was a massive failure of foresight. Not a single one of these studies gave even a hint that a major systemic change might be just around the corner.

Only rarely did anyone in these five journals try to peer forward, to anticipate possible crises in the future, and even these efforts were limited mostly to individual economies rather than to risks for the system as a whole. Illustrative was a perceptive study by a pair of US scholars (Leblang and Satyanath 2006), who focused on linkages among domestic political institutions, financial market expectations, and the onset of currency crises. Institutional variables such as divided government or government turnover, the two researchers argued, were likely to heighten the variance of expectations among speculators and thus heighten the chance of a run on a country's money. The paper's aim was to improve on the ability of standard economic models to forecast national currency crises. But that is hardly the same thing as contemplating the possibility of radical transformation on a regional or global scale.

There were occasional exceptions, of course. Helleiner argues that "the record of the field was not entirely dismal ... A number of IPE scholars did correctly identify many of the key market and regulatory failures that ended up contributing to the crisis" (Helleiner 2011b: 83). Similarly, Joscha Wullweber, a young German scholar, contends that "A closer examination of relevant literature ... shows that already before the start of the crisis, there was a robust body of pluralist studies and analyses with clear evidence that pointed towards crisis-related tendencies" (Wullweber 2019: 301). But as Wullweber's careful phrasing suggests, these exceptions were just that – exceptional. They required exhaustive search and were not easy to find. As Helleiner (2011b: 84) acknowledges, most of these exceptions could better be described as part of John Ravenhill's "missing middle." They were certainly not representative of the broad mainstream of orthodox IPE scholarship.

Overall, therefore, it is abundantly clear that the pathology of inadvertent omission was rife. Most members of the American school remained placidly oblivious to the coming storm. Remarkably, few even felt any responsibility to warn that clouds might be gathering. As Layna Mosley and David Singer, two prominent US scholars, wrote defensively, IPE researchers "are generally not in the business of predicting financial crises or recessions, and so the field is unlikely to see the crisis as a manifestation of scholarly failure" (Mosley and Singer 2009: 420).

Heterodoxy

Among scholars of a more critical persuasion, by contrast, the story was otherwise. In Britain in particular, there were actually quite a few researchers who foresaw the possibility of a major structural crisis in finance. Many took their inspiration from Susan Strange, whose concerns before her untimely death were well articulated in two memorable books, *Casino Capitalism* (1986) and *Mad Money* (1998). The titles say it all. "Gamblers in the casino," she wrote, "have got out of hand, almost beyond, it sometimes seems, the control of governments" (1986: 21). With the rise of largely unregulated capital markets, finance was going mad. The global system was becoming more and more fragile, worryingly vulnerable to bouts of speculation and instability. A debilitating crash, Strange contended, was just a matter of time. Others, following in her footsteps, developed the theme in greater detail, emphasizing the need for ameliorative actions before it was too late (Langley 2002; Blyth 2003; Watson 2007). Here there was little hesitation to predict a financial shock.

That does not mean that heterodox scholars were unusually prescient. Predictions were loosely framed and often maddingly imprecise. Few analysts foresaw the specific sequence of events that ultimately unfolded; many were downright wrong about the details; certainly none got the timing right. In many ways they invited comparison with the mythical boy who cried wolf. In 2008, their fears turned out to be justified: the wolf did indeed make an appearance, threatening to bring down the whole edifice of global finance. But what about all the times before that when forecasts of the wolf's menacing arrival turned out to be premature? A vague generalized apprehension is no substitute for keenly detailed analysis.

Nonetheless, heterodoxy's sense of the larger picture cannot be denied. In anxious ruminations, the threat of a looming crisis was palpable. No one reading the critical literature at the time could say that they were not warned. Feeling vindicated, therefore, many critical scholars have enjoyed a pleasurable moment of *schadenfreude* at the expense of their more orthodox colleagues. Don't blame us, they seem to say. It was the other guys who missed the signs. In a formal response to Queen Elizabeth's question, the British Academy (2009) spoke of a "failure of collective imagination of many bright people." Evidently seeking to be tactful, the response declined to name names. But between the lines it was evident that it was the American school that the Academy had in mind – scholars who have "difficulty ... seeing the risk to the system as a whole [and] frequently lose sight of the bigger picture." A flattering contrast is drawn with others – quite obviously, more heterodox research-ers – who "did foresee the crisis ... There were many warnings."

Less tactful was a subsequent addendum to the Academy's response submitted by ten noted scholars (Dow et al. 2009). For them, the problem was worse. It was "a preoccupation with a narrow range of formal tech-niques" – a frequent criticism of the American school. "The preference for mathematical technique over real-world substances diverted many [scholars] from looking at the vital whole ... What has been scarce is a professional wisdom informed by a rich knowledge of psychology, institutional structures and historical precedents" – hallmarks of the "open range" that Susan Strange had long championed.

Overall, rebukes like these have become commonplace in heterodox post mortems following the crisis. Representative are the words of Ronen Palan, a well-known British researcher, writing of the events that led up to the GFC. "The American school failed to appreciate these developments," he declared. "Was it an accident? I do not think so" (Palan 2011: 189). For critical theorists the crisis was no "Black Swan" event that few could have foreseen. Rather it was, as one source put it, more of a "Lame Duck problem where theory itself is the culprit" (Blyth and Matthijs 2017: 205). The failures of orthodoxy, in the eyes of their more radical counterparts, were intrinsic, an unavoidable consequence of serious paradigmatic flaws. Most critical theorists blame the tendency of

US-style IPE to mimic the general theoretical orientation of mainstream economics, with its core emphases on incremental change and equilibrium assumptions (Palan 2011; Green and Hay 2015). The opposition to the American style is overt and unmistakable.

NON-REMEDIES

What remedies might there be for the twin pathologies of inadvertent omission and overt opposition? One possibility, in principle, might simply be to promote what in the social sciences is known as a "corner" solution. The choice among possible remedies may be thought of as a maximization problem: a function to be maximized. Typically, all elements of a maximized function are assumed to be variable, with trade-offs negotiated among them. A corner solution is a special answer to the maximization problem in which the value of one of the elements is held constant and set equal to zero.

In our context, two such options come to mind, both quite radical. In one corner is the option of *singularism* – compression of the field to just a single uniform paradigm, a standard model that would be shared by all. The problem of diversity would be resolved by *eliminating* diversity. In effect, diversity would be set at zero. In the other corner would be *subdivision* – a permanent partition of IPE's invisible college into a plurality of new and distinctive successor fields of study, each with markedly less within-type variance. The problem of diversity would be resolved by *surrendering* to diversity. Here it is the field's unity that would be set at zero. In practice, however, neither of these approaches can be counted upon to be effective or even viable. They are, in reality, non-remedies.

The advantages of singularism are easy to comprehend. No longer would there have to be contentious debate over the characteristics that collectively differentiate one theoretical perspective from another. No longer would time be wasted on explaining assumptions or defining terms. Instead, discussion could now focus exclusively on the substance of analytical puzzles, without the distraction of paradigm war. This happy vision is what Lake (2006) had in mind when he spoke hopefully about "Kuhnian normalcy" and the "maturing" of IPE in the US. In effect, he contended, singularism was taking over. For US scholars, the field was becoming centered on a single "hegemonic approach." Though in writing these words he was careful to make clear that he was speaking mainly of the orthodox style of IPE, it was evident that he would not have been saddened to see OEP's emerging dominance of the American school extend to other parts of the invisible college as well.

But that reckons without singularism's disadvantages, which are considerable. These include the familiar risks of omitted-variable bias, under-specified models, and general desiccation of the field. In addition, there are also difficult practical questions. First is the issue of just what to include in the standard model. The Big Picture of IPE today, as we have seen, encompasses a vast array of sharply contrasting theoretical perspectives, all stubbornly defended. To satisfy IPE's many factions, a myriad of considerations of all kinds would have to be stuffed into a single analytical framework. Any hope of theoretical or conceptual parsimony would be lost. It is not even clear that such a consolidation would be workable. And second is the issue of how, in practical terms, we might actually manage the transition from today's rich pluralism to universal consensus on one agreed replacement. Who would have to make concessions, and what would they be expected to give up? Even more crucially, who would decide? Academic life, as I have already noted, is highly rivalrous. It defies imagination to think that somehow all of today's stresses could be suppressed for long on behalf of one universal vision. Singularism may have some appeal in principle, but it is unlikely to be feasible in practice. In short, it is a non-starter.

The advantages of subdivision are equally easy to comprehend. No longer would we have to fear an outbreak of civil war in IPE. No longer would time be wasted on Great Debates. Instead, there would now be amicable divorce similar to the split that divided economics and political science in the late nineteenth century. Once and for all, as Lake put it, we could "simply get on with the business." But that happy vision too is questionable, for two reasons. For one thing, a partition of the invisible college is no guarantee of an enduring "peace for our time," to recall British Prime Minister Neville Chamberlain's notorious claim after the fateful Munich conference of 1938. As Europe discovered the next year, a truce without genuine reconciliation might prove sadly fragile and fleeting. Hostilities between discourse coalitions might not be annulled but merely postponed. In time, new within-type variances might easily emerge as scholars, legitimately concerned about their professional advancement, again seek to differentiate their own contributions from others. And for another thing, the approach would make it even more difficult for cohorts to cultivate mutual understanding across factional lines. Instead, new Great Walls of silence might well emerge, curtailing opportunities for force multiplication and impoverishing IPE research in general. For both reasons, this option too must be regarded as a non-starter.

REMEDIES

Are there any better remedies – prescriptions that might actually work? The challenge for IPE here is twofold. It is to encourage mutual understanding across the field's many "networks and niches" while at the same time discouraging outbreaks of bitter paradigm war. The former would maximize the blessing of force multiplication. The latter would minimize the curse of potential conflict. The key to the first is minimizing the risk of inadvertent omission. The key to the second is minimizing the risk of overt opposition.

Clearly, all that calls for a delicate calculus and is not likely to be achieved easily. On the one hand, anything that seeks to dissolve the barriers between silos risks arousing frictions and enmity. The more we learn about alternative perspectives, the more grounds we may find for overt opposition. On the other hand, anything that seeks to reduce the danger of paradigm war risks foregoing opportunities for mutual enrichment. The more we try to suppress conflict, the more grounds we may find for simply sticking with our own kind. Is there a satisfactory solution to this tricky challenge?

Metaphors

There are no easy answers. In my own early efforts to ponder the question, I borrowed the image of "bridge-building" from Susan Strange. Back in her "Mutual Neglect" manifesto (Strange 1970), as noted in Chapter 1, Strange called for a "new generation of bridge-builders" to close the gap between the specialities of international economics and international relations. Much could be gained, she insisted, by learning from one another. Inspired by her example, I used the same metaphor in my *Intellectual History* (Cohen 2008) to address the myopic gaps between the American and British versions of IPE. The two schools, I argued, were really quite complementary, the strengths of one largely balancing the weaknesses of the other. So why not see what could be discovered from each, for their mutual gain? Others who have made use of the bridge metaphor include UK-based scholars Richard Higgott and Matthew Watson (Higgott and Watson 2008) and Phil Cerny (2009).

Along similar lines, Kevin Young, a Canadian based in the US, has called for a new "engaged pluralism" to replace the more "alienated pluralism" that regrettably characterizes IPE today (Young 2021). The notion of "alienated pluralism" highlights the downside of diversity – the insular tribalism of the invisible college's many factions, each stubbornly barricaded in its own silo. Communication across paradigmatic lines is discouraged, and knowledge is fragmented. For Young, the solution lies in conversion to a more "engaged pluralism" that "would retain the diversity of IPE's many approaches and traditions but would promise greater knowledge synthesis." What is needed, he argues, is a new "scientific ethos," which he defines as "a characteristic cultural orientation, manifest in beliefs, practices and aspirations." Our collective aim should be "to encourage a broader and more rigorous engagement with one another's work."

Not everyone agrees that such engagement is possible or even desirable. Mark Blyth is particularly adamant, wondering "if a bridge can, or indeed should be built between such radically different things" (Blyth 2011: 136). But it is difficult to see what harm could be done by trying. Surely there may be benefit in seeking to understand what other cohorts are doing, and why.

But that is not enough. Bridge-building and engaged pluralism are handy (and hardy) metaphors. Numerous colleagues have expressed to me in private correspondence what they see as a need for more conversation among research traditions in IPE. But what, specifically, are these metaphors meant to convey beyond a worthy open-mindedness? Behind their superficial appeal, their practical content is obscure – a kind of verbal Potemkin village. I have come to believe that if we are to be serious about rethinking diversity in IPE, we must be more precise about just what bridges may be built and what elements of pluralism may be engaged.

Analytic Eclecticism

To my mind, the most convincing effort to develop a prescription along these lines has come from Peter Katzenstein and a colleague of his, Rudra Sil (Sil and Katzenstein 2010a, 2010b). Their aim is to find a way to cope comfortably with the confusing diversity (not to say cacophony) of a field of study like IPE. Scholars, they write, must "resist the temptation to assume that one or another research tradition is inherently superior" (2010b: 2). Instead, we must be prepared to go "beyond paradigms" to look for hidden "commonalities" and "connections" among seemingly incommensurable models. A multiplicity of perspectives should be understood not as a burden to be deplored but as an opportunity to expand and enrich research. The approach is labeled *analytic eclecticism.* In their words:

> Analytic eclecticism is about making intellectually and practically useful con-
> nections among clusters of analyses that are substantively related but normally
> formulated in separate paradigms ... It challenges the analytic boundaries
> derived from paradigmatic assumptions, and refuses to carve up complex
> social phenomena solely for the purpose of making them more tractable to
> a particular style of analysis ... The goal is not to synthesize, subsume, or
> replace paradigms. It is to demonstrate the practical relevance of, and substan-
> tive connections among, theories and narratives constructed within seemingly
> discrete and irreconcilable approaches. (2010b: 2–3)

The key to analytic eclecticism is *disaggregation* – picking apart diverse paradigms in a search for useful force multipliers. The gravest draw-back of metaphors like bridge-building and engaged pluralism is the implication that competing theoretical approaches must be compared or contrasted *in their entirety.* Broad perspectives must go head-to-head. But in reality we know that paradigms are not holistic but multidimen-sional, each a unique amalgam of features that collectively distinguish one school of thought from another. Research traditions may seem totally at odds when each is considered in the aggregate, yet when disaggregated may reveal new opportunities to augment practical understanding – a new menu of options. On the one hand, gaps may be closed by sewing together a variety of elements from diverse paradigms. That seems to be what Sil and Katzenstein mean by connections. On the other hand, new insight may be gained by integrating together different interpretations of a single key element, which appears to be what Sil and Katzenstein mean by commonalities. Either way, what looks like outright combat among competing styles may, in fact, turn out to contain the seeds for peaceful reconciliation – force multiplication at work.

Analytic eclecticism is not without its critics, of course. This is the academic world, after all. Debate comes naturally. Some comments focus on the incoherence that could result from an attempt to integrate concepts or characteristics derived from very different intellectual traditions. Others worry about a potential loss of parsimony that could make new theory-building cumbersome. But neither objection is fatal. As Sil and Katzenstein respond reasonably, it would not be impossible to rely on "translation and redefinition" to avoid incoherence and preserve parsimony (2010a: 414).

In developing their ideas, Sil and Katzenstein were most concerned about the study of world politics. Their target audience was to be found among specialists of IR where according to a recent president of the International Studies Association, their strategy has been "gaining ground" (James 2019: 782). But as the two scholars suggest, there is no reason to think that their argument might not be applicable to IPE as well. "By making connections between paradigms that are typically disengaged from one another," they insist, "analytic eclecticism holds promise for enhancing our understanding of different facets of the global political economy" (Sil and Katzenstein 2010b: 110). Here, I submit, is where we might find the remedy that we need for the twin pathologies of inadvertent omission and overt opposition.

CONNECTIONS AND COMMONALITIES

To put analytic eclecticism to work in practical terms, we need to identify the elements of IPE's diverse paradigms that seem most likely to offer the connections and commonalities that Sil and Katzenstein have in mind. The two scholars themselves propose several useful examples that they regard as models of eclectic analysis for IPE. These include studies by several European-based scholars and one Canadian. Notably, they offer no example from the US, demonstrating once again the unfortunate parochialism of the American school. For the most part, US researchers (or researchers trained in the US tradition) feel little compulsion to explore what other schools of thought are doing.

However, it is notable that in each of the examples provided by Sil and Katzenstein, it is connections, not commonalities, that receive the lion's share of attention. *The Social Sources of Financial Power*, by Leonard Seabrooke (2006), is praised for an analytical framework that "incorporates mechanisms from different traditions in diverse fields of scholarship" (Sil and Katzenstein 2010b: 112). Similarly, *The New Masters of Capital*, by Tim Sinclair (2005) is complimented for its use of "tracking processes that reflect back on a number of different theoretical orientations" (Sil and Katzenstein 2010b: 120–1). In all their cases, it is the tapestry woven from disparate threads that is highlighted: a first element from one paradigm, another from a second paradigm, and so on. Commonalities, by contrast, are most conspicuous by their absence.

Can we offer some possible commonalities? I believe so. In the Big Picture I painted earlier, I stressed five attributes to distinguish among alternative paradigms – ontology, agenda, purpose, boundaries, and epistemology. Purpose has already been discussed in the previous chapter, and agenda will be addressed in the next. But that still leaves three defining characteristics. All three, I believe, look like prime candidates for going "beyond paradigms."

Ontology

Ontology, we know, is about units of analysis. Who are the key actors, and what are their relationships? Choices range from individual persons, as in Everyday IPE, to social classes as in the Marxist tradition; to the sovereign state as in the American school; to broader world-systems or world orders as in diverse system-level theories. Considered holistically, these diverse ontologies appear to be incompatible, utterly alien from one another. They seem to be communicating in entirely different languages – a veritable Tower of Babel.

But what if we translate units of analysis into corresponding units of time? Years ago, Helleiner (1997), drawing on the earlier scholarship of the renowned French historian Fernand Braudel, suggested that the functioning of the world economy may be thought of as an historical process incorporating at least three distinct time perspectives. At one extreme is the *longue durée* of centuries during which fundamental systemic transformation is shaped by deep social forces. The pace of change is gradual if not glacial. At the other extreme is *l'histoire événementielle*, contemporary existence, in which actors of all kinds – from individuals to governments to transnational agents – are engaged daily in reacting to or seeking to cope with events in real time. And in between is the "episodic" or "conjunctural" dimension, measured in years or even decades, where there may be much change *within* social systems but not necessarily change *of* social systems – changes of degree but not necessarily of kind.

It seems plausible to assume that during each of these three timescales, different actors will take center stage. In the short term of *l'histoire événementielle*, we can expect outcomes to be driven most by everyday folk, interest groups, and other subnational or transnational constituencies. These would be the proper units of analysis. But in the medium term of "episodic" or "conjunctural" developments, by contrast, the sovereign state would seem to play the most critical role; while in the *longue durée* it is the larger system itself that logically becomes the focus of attention.

The diverse paradigms in IPE's Tower of Babel may rest on very different ontologies, yet there clearly is a commonality that links them all. It is the commonality of time. Each perspective embodies its own conception of time. With this commonality in mind, an eclectic analysis could be constructed incorporating multiple units of analysis. Imagine, for example, a theoretical model of the world economy comprised of three interlocking tracks moving at different speeds – fast for the track representing *l'histoire événementielle*, slower for the conjunctural track, and slowest of all for the *longue durée*. Clearly, interactions across the three tracks could be expected to be numerous and complex. The potential research questions, therefore, are practically endless. At any given time, how much has to happen on the fast track before it results in sustained change on the conjunctural track? Likewise, how much change will be tolerated *within* the broader system before it becomes a change *of* the system – a genuine transformation? How long will all these things take? And are there inertias or feedback loops that might be expected to alter the sequence or timing of events?

Questions like these are asked all the time in the real world, though not always using the formal terminology of Fernand Braudel. Consider, for instance, the notorious aphorism of John Maynard Keynes, first uttered a century ago, that "In the long run we are all dead" (Keynes 1924: 80). Many have understood those words to mean that we can forget about the longer-term effects of decisions made in the short term. Just concentrate on the present, *l'histoire événementielle*. But that would be a mistake. Keynes, one of the most influential economists of the last century, was worldly enough to recognize that time works on multiple tracks. A series of minor marginal changes may cumulatively result in major transformation. But for Keynes it was a matter of priorities. In the midst of a deep economic downturn, he had no patience for conservative economists who benignly assumed that all would be well in the long run. "The long run," he declared, "is a misleading guide to current affairs" (Keynes 1924: 80). While waiting for equilibrium to return, he warned, many people might well starve to death. In the absence of speedier recovery, therefore, immediate government action seemed the wiser choice. This early intuition was subsequently formalized by Keynes in 1936 in his justly famous *General Theory of Employment, Interest and Money*, universally hailed as the founding cornerstone of the branch of the economics discipline known today as macroeconomics.

But one does not have to be a Keynes to see the opportunity for force multiplication in translating ontology into time. In place of pitched battles between competing paradigms, commonalities can be highlighted to enhance understanding. Translators would no longer be needed on the Tower of Babel.

Boundaries

Boundaries are about where we draw lines between the models and perspectives of our own specialty and other scholarly disciplines. In the words of one recent discussion, "boundary work involves those practices and mechanisms of inclusion and exclusion, recognition and misrecognition, remembering and forgetting that continually draw boundaries around what is legitimate IPE and what is not" (Clift et al. 2021). Boundaries are important because they determine the range of perspectives that will be admitted to analysis. For some scholars, mostly to be found in the American school, the lines should be drawn narrowly. Nothing more should be admitted for research purposes than the analytical tools of IPE's two most immediate antecedents – economics and political science. All other disciplinary traditions can be excluded. For other scholars, more in the spirit of Susan Strange (1984, 1991), the range should be "unfenced," open to all. In addressing the How question, the field should be as inclusive as possible.

To a limited degree, opinion in the field may be moving in the direction of greater theoretical openness – but *only* to a limited degree. Privately, a good number of colleagues have expressed to me frustration with the long-standing reluctance of many in the invisible college to see what other established research traditions might have to offer. Fences, increasingly, are bemoaned rather than celebrated. The sentiment was especially evident at a 2019 conference in Berlin organized by the editors of *International Organization* – considered by many to be the flagship journal of the American school – to celebrate the publication's 75th anniversary. Nearly a dozen-and-a-half research papers, addressing a broad spectrum of topics, were presented by leading scholars, to be published later in a special issue of the periodical. Said one participant: "My sense is that the field was curious about a lot of things." However, it was also evident that curiosity did not necessarily lead to action. As the same participant continued, the field may want to know more about "things" but judging from the work discussed in Berlin, it is "strangely unread about them." In practical terms, the field is still littered with fences.

The differences are not inconsequential. At stake is the all-important question of authority. Who shall speak for the field? Who gets to define which approaches are intellectually acceptable? Many a battle has been fought over these questions. Not surprisingly, those who continue to favor strict narrow boundaries come mainly from the specialties of international economics and IR. What seems more natural than to limit admissibility to those who represent either the "P" or the "E" in IPE? Conversely, it is hardly surprising that those who fight for a more open range tend mostly to have backgrounds that are rooted in other related areas of scholarship. These might include close cognate fields of study such as comparative politics or global studies or first cousins like sociology or history. Or they might encompass as well even more distant relatives ranging from geography or anthropology to gender and racial studies. Conflicts over authority, regrettably, are bound to become personal, since professional standing and its rewards are ultimately at stake. No wonder, then, that such polemics so often seem to end up looking like religious war. Other established fields of study have split apart over less.

Fragmentation is not inevitable, however. Once again, analytical eclecticism might come to the rescue. Boundaries represent a key commonality. Just as each perspective embodies its own conception of time, every paradigm is built, implicitly or explicitly, on some understanding of IPE's legitimate intellectual space. The differences are real. But suppose we treat each perspective not as an adversary to be contested but rather as something more like a useful tool to test for robustness. Study of any particular topic could begin, as it typically does, with a certain sense of boundaries in mind. Research might be framed in the familiar terms of economics and political science; or alternatively in terms that draw on theoretical approaches borrowed from other disciplines or specialities. But before concluding, the researcher should be expected to go on to ask: Is there anything missing? Is there anything that needs to be qualified? Would the results be different if boundaries were redrawn? The more scholars test the robustness of their analytical path in this manner, the more persuasive they will be in promoting their conclusions.

Epistemology

Epistemology, finally, is about methods and the grounds for learning. We know from earlier chapters that methodology is one of the most conspicuous of all the divisive problems of IPE, drawing a bright red line between the two sides of the orthodox/heterodox divide. On the orthodox side, most factions believe methods should be as "scientific" as possible. Only the most rigorous quantitative or qualitative modes of analysis will do. On the heterodox side, by contrast, many researchers denounce such a strict credo as little more than a "methods fetish." Handled properly, theorists insist, other less formal techniques might be equally productive. Research, whether mainstream or radical, that does not meet some faction's "methodological litmus test" will be condemned to suffer the ultimate penalties – inadvertent omission or overt opposition.

Each side has a point. A hard science model, based on the twin principles of positivism and empiricism, may be something of a fetish but does hold out the promise of considerable precision and clarity. Conversely, the more interpretive approaches favored on the heterodox side may not always meet the highest of analytical norms but do offer a fuller appreciation of the human condition. I am reminded of a time when I was invited to speak to a group of visitors to my university along with a faculty member from the chemistry department. Asked about his relations with students, my colleague spoke of his office hours when he and students could discuss formulas and equations. In turn, I jokingly added that in the social sciences we too have office hours, except in our case we typically use not numbers but words. And he in turn replied, with a wicked smile: "Yes, and that is what we in the hard sciences call ambiguity." The riposte was perfect. The contrast between our two views of methodology could not have been more vividly illuminated.

In reality, of course, neither side is beyond criticism. The hypothetico-deductivism of an applied scientific method rests on the assumption that social phenomena are amenable to explanation in essentially the same manner as are natural phenomena. Hence the same principles of positivism and empiricism that are employed to isolate causal mechanisms in the physical sciences can be applied to the study of social relations as well. Universal truths are out there, mathematically unimpeachable, just waiting to be discovered. John Kenneth Galbraith, one of America's most prominent economists in the mid-twentieth century, labeled the approach "imitative scientism" – a faithful replication of the methods of the natural sciences (Galbraith 1970). But replication, strictly speaking, requires an ability to conduct controlled experiments, repeating the same analysis over and over again in order to ratify results. In the social sciences, obviously, iterations like that are simply not possible. Every moment is a sample of one. For Susan Strange, that made the hard science approach "phoney science, not social science" (1994: 217).

Conversely, the more relaxed nature of historical-relativist paradigms on the heterodox side can be criticized for their tendency to mix objective analysis and normative judgments, thereby making generalization difficult and the cumulation of knowledge virtually impossible. Informal methodology does not have to mean a compromise of scholarly standards. Greater reliance on intuition or inference certainly does not mean that analytical rigor must be abandoned. As Palan (2011) insists, heterodox scholars on the whole are every bit as committed to careful analysis of empirical evidence as are their mainstream peers. But there is no doubt that as compared with a hard science model, conclusions on the heterodox side by and large tend to be more conjectural and contingent. It is difficult to reduce their subjective observations to a concise set of logical theorems.

But nothing of this means that either type of epistemology is without utility. Both research strategies have long proved their worth, even if neither on its own can be expected to be beyond challenge. So why not seize an opportunity for force multiplication, in a manner similar to what I just proposed for the element of boundaries. Like time and boundaries, methodology too can be treated as a commonality. Every analysis is built on a preferred methodology. So here too analysis might start with one methodology but then put a second or third to work for the purpose of robustness testing. To some extent, we already see a trend in IPE toward more and more use of "mixed methods." But, regrettably, most often that simply involves two or more variants from the same side of the orthodox/heterodox divide (for example, a big-N regression analysis followed by a couple of carefully structured case studies). Researchers need to look further afield for more unfamiliar methodologies that might prove to be useful.

CONCLUSION

The aim of this chapter has been to think anew about the abundant diversity of the field of IPE. Though pluralism can be a blessing, today it is more often a curse, exposing the field to the twin-like pathologies of inadvertent omission and overt opposition. Effective remedies are not easy to find. Radical corner solutions like singularism (compression to one uniform paradigm) or subdivision (formal partition) must be considered non-starters. Likewise, metaphors like build-bridging or engaged pluralism have superficial appeal but lack much practical content. The key to the dilemma is not to deplore diversity but rather to make the best possible use of it. Most promising is a strategy that builds on the notion of analytic eclecticism proposed by Sil and Katzenstein. The idea is to go "beyond paradigms" by looking for hidden commonalities and connections among competing theories and models. Examples of successful connections are provided by Sil and Katzenstein. Further possibilities were offered in this chapter emphasizing commonalities among ontologies, boundaries, and epistemologies. Gaining widespread adoption of analytic eclecticism, however, will not be easy. As in the previous chapter, the all-important practicalities of implementation will be postponed until the final chapter.

REFERENCES

Blyth, Mark (2003), "The Political Power of Financial Ideas: Transparency, Risk, and Distribution in Global Finance," in Jonathan Kirshner, ed., *Monetary Orders: Ambiguous Economics, Ubiquitous Politics* (Ithaca, NY: Cornell University Press), 239–59.

Blyth, Mark (2011), "Torn Between Two Lovers? Caught in the Middle of British and American IPE," in Nicola Phillips and Catherine E. Weaver, eds., *International Political Economy: Debating the Past, Present and Future* (London and New York: Routledge), 133–40.

Blyth, Mark and Matthias Matthijs (2017), "Black Swans, Lame Ducks, and the Mystery of IPE's Missing Macroeconomy," *Review of International Political Economy* 24:2, 203–31.

British Academy (2009), Letter to Her Majesty the Queen, July 22.

Broz, J. Lawrence (2005), "Congressional Politics of International Financial Rescues," *American Journal of Political Science* 49:3, 479–96.

Burnham, Peter (1994), "Open Marxism and Vulgar International Political Economy," *Review of International Political Economy* 1:2, 221–31.

Cerny, Philip (2009), "Bridging the Transatlantic Divide? Toward a Structurational Approach to International Political Economy," in Mark Blyth, ed., *The Routledge Handbook of IPE: IPE as a Global Conversation* (London and New York: Routledge), 140–59.

Clift, Ben, Peter M. Kristensen, and Ben Rosamond (2021), "Remembering and Forgetting IPE: Disciplinary History as Boundary Work," *Review of International Political Economy* (forthcoming).

Cohen, Benjamin J. (2004), *The Future of Money* (Princeton, NJ: Princeton University Press).

Cohen, Benjamin J. (2008), *International Political Economy: An Intellectual History* (Princeton, NJ: Princeton University Press).

Cohen, Benjamin J. (2009), "A Grave Case of Myopia," *International Interactions* 35:4, 436–44.

Cohen, Benjamin J. (2017), "The IPE of Money Revisited," *Review of International Political Economy* 24:4, 657–80.

Cohen, Benjamin J. (2019), *Advanced Introduction to International Political Economy*, revised 2nd edition (Cheltenham, UK and Northampton, MA, USA: Edward Elgar Publishing).

Dow, Sheila C. and nine others (2009), Letter to Her Majesty the Queen, August 15.

Farrell, Henry and Abraham Newman (2016), "The New Interdependence Approach: Theoretical Developments and Empirical Demonstration," *Review of International Political Economy* 23:5, 713–36.

Galbraith, John Kenneth (1970), *Economics, Peace, and Laughter* (Harmondsworth, UK: Penguin).

Green, Jeremy and Colin Hay (2015), "Towards a New Political Economy of the Crisis: Getting What Went Wrong Right," *New Political Economy* 20:3, 331–41.

Grieco, Joseph M. (2019), "The Schools of Thought Problem in International Relations," *International Studies Review* 21:3, 424–46.

Helleiner, Eric (1997), "Braudelian Reflections on Economic Globalization: The Historian as Pioneer," in Stephen R. Gill and James H. Mittleman, eds., *Innovation and Transformation in International Studies* (Cambridge: Cambridge University Press), 90–104.

Helleiner, Eric (2011a), "Division and Dialogue in Anglo-American IPE: A Reluctant Canadian View," in Nicola Phillips and Catherine E. Weaver, eds., *International Political Economy: Debating the Past, Present and Future* (London and New York: Routledge), 178–84.

Helleiner, Eric (2011b), "Understanding the 2007–2008 Global Financial Crisis: Lessons for Scholars of International Political Economy," *Annual Review of Political Science* 14, 67–87.

Hicken, Allen, Shanker Satyanath, and Ernest Sergenti (2005), "Political Institutions and Economic Performance: The Effects of Accountability and Obstacles to Policy Change," *American Journal of Political Science* 49:4 (October), 897–907.

Higgott, Richard and Matthew Watson (2008), "All at Sea in a Barbed Wire Canoe: Professor Cohen's Transatlantic Voyage in IPE," *Review of International Political Economy* 15:1, 1–17.

James, Patrick (2019), "Systemist International Relations," *International Studies Quarterly* 63:4, 781–804.

Keefer, Philip (2007), "Elections, Special Interests, and Financial Crisis," *International Organization* 61:3, 607–41.

Keynes, John Maynard (1924), *A Tract on Monetary Reform* (London: Macmillan).

Lake, David A. (2006), "International Political Economy: A Maturing Interdiscipline," in Barry R. Weingast and Donald A. Wittman, eds., *Oxford Handbook of Political Economy* (New York: Oxford University Press), 757–77.

Lake, David A. (2011), "TRIPS Across the Atlantic: Theory and Epistemology in IPE," in Nicola Phillips and Catherine E. Weaver, eds., *International Political Economy: Debating the Past, Present and Future* (London and New York: Routledge), 45–52.

Lake, David A. (2018), "International Legitimacy Lost? Rule and Resistance when America is First," *Perspectives on Politics* 16:1, 7–21.

Langley, Paul (2002), *World Financial Orders: An Historical International Political Economy* (London: Routledge).

Leblang, David and Shanker Satyanath (2006), "Institutions, Expectations, and Currency Crises," *International Organization* 60:1, 245–62.

Mosley, Layna and David Andrew Singer (2009), "The Global Financial Crisis: Lessons and Opportunities for International Political Economy," *International Interactions* 35:4, 420–9.

Oatley, Thomas H. (2011), "The Reductionist Gamble: Open Economy Politics in the Global Economy," *International Organization* 65:2, 311–41.

Palan, Ronen (2011), "The Proof of the Pudding is in the Eating: IPE in the Light of the Crisis of 2007/8," in Nicola Phillips and Catherine E. Weaver, eds., *International Political Economy: Debating the Past, Present and Future* (London and New York: Routledge), 185–93.

Pepinsky, Thomas B. (2008), "Capital Mobility and Coalitional Politics: Authoritarian Regimes and Economic Adjustment in Southeast Asia," *World Politics* 60:3, 438–74.

Rosas, Guillermo (2006), "Bagehot or Bailout? An Analysis of Government Responses to Banking Crises," *American Journal of Political Science* 50:1, 175–91.

Seabrooke, Leonard (2006), *The Social Sources of Financial Power: Domestic Legitimacy and International Financial Orders* (Ithaca, NY: Cornell University Press).

Sil, Rudra and Peter J. Katzenstein (2010a), "Analytic Eclecticism in the Study of World Politics: Reconfiguring Problems and Mechanisms across Research Traditions," *Perspectives on Politics* 8:2, 411–31.

Sil, Rudra and Peter J. Katzenstein (2010b), *Beyond Paradigms: Analytical Eclecticism in the Study of World Politics* (New York: Palgrave Macmillan).

Sinclair, Timothy J. (2005), *The New Masters of Capital: American Bond Rating Agencies and the Politics of Creditworthiness* (Ithaca, NY: Cornell University Press).

Strange, Susan (1970), "International Economics and International Relations: A Case of Mutual Neglect," *International Affairs* 46:2, 304–15.

Strange, Susan (1984), "Preface," in Susan Strange, ed., *Paths to International Political Economy* (London: George Allen & Unwin), ix–xi.

Strange, Susan (1986), *Casino Capitalism* (Oxford: Basil Blackwell).

Strange, Susan (1991), "An Eclectic Approach," in Craig N. Murphy and Roger Tooze, eds., *The New International Political Economy* (Boulder, CO: Lynne Rienner), 33–49.

Strange, Susan (1994), "Wake Up, Krasner! The World *Has* Changed," *Review of International Political Economy* 1:2, 209–19.

Strange, Susan (1998), *Mad Money* (Manchester: Manchester University Press).

Vivares, Ernesto (2020), "Global Conversations and Inquiries," in Ernesto Vivares, ed., *The Routledge Handbook to Global Political Economy* (New York and London: Routledge), 9–25.

Walter, Andrew (2016), "Open Economy Politics and International Security Dynamics: Explaining International Cooperation in Financial Crises," *European Journal of International Relations* 22:2, 289–312.

Watson, Matthew (2007), *The Political Economy of International Capital Mobility* (Basingstoke, UK: Palgrave Macmillan).

Weaver, Catherine E. (2011), "IPE's Split Brain," in Nicola Phillips and Catherine E. Weaver, eds., *International Political Economy: Debating the Past, Present and Future* (London and New York: Routledge), 141–9.

Widmaier, Wesley (2016), *Economic Ideas in Political Time* (Cambridge, UK: Cambridge University Press).

Wullweber, Joscha (2019), "Monism vs. Pluralism, the Global Financial Crisis, and the Methodological Struggle in the Field of International Political Economy," *Competition and Change* 23:3, 287–311.

Young, Kevin L. (2021), "Progress, Pluralism and Science: Moving from Alienated to Engaged Pluralism," *Review of International Political Economy* 28:2, 406-20.

5. Rethinking agenda

Finally, we arrive at the What question: What issues should we address in International Political Economy (IPE)? What is the field's proper agenda? As a practical matter, there is no end to the number of problems and puzzles in the global economy that would seem to call out for attention. Our challenge, as scholars, is to rethink what range of questions we might realistically aspire to answer through our study of IPE. Should we limit our research narrowly to what I have suggested may be considered the irreducible core of the field – the "P" of politics and the "E" of economics? Or should we expand our horizons to take in ever more distant considerations, drawing on a wider orbit of other disciplines and specialties? The limits of IPE's agenda are endlessly debated by specialists, adding to tensions already generated by fights over purpose and diversity (Clift et al. 2021). This too can be considered a grievous pathology, which we might call "boundary battles."

In principle, of course, there ought to be no limits at all. Intellectual inquiry should know no bounds. You never know when significant value might be added. In practice, however, it is obvious that our field cannot pretend to offer useful instruction on every possible subject. No Grand IPE Theory of Everything is possible. Nothing should be rejected *a priori*. But we must accept that in many cases, maybe even most, the marginal value of a new departure could turn out to be trivial or even non-existent. Almost certainly there will be limits to what issues the field can confront with any degree of insight. Our task, in rethinking IPE, is to work out what those limits might be. Much depends on the previous Why and How questions. What is the purpose of our scholarship and what theoretical approaches do we have at our disposal?

DISCONTENT

Discontent with the coverage of the field today is widespread among IPE scholars. As individuals, each of us may be quite satisfied with the research agenda that we have set for ourselves. Personal pride and professional reputations are enhanced by continuously refining our expertise on a select set of issues. But that does not rule out a high degree of dis-satisfaction with the direction taken by the field as a whole – with what everyone else is doing. Increasingly, anxiety is expressed about yawning gaps in what the invisible college is undertaking collectively. Why else would there be so many efforts, as described back in Chapter 2, to extend the frontiers of the field in one direction or another? Boundary battles erupt frequently. The sense of many is that key elements are missing. IPE, it is said, has abdicated its responsibility to address major issues of practical real-world importance.

Anxiety along these lines was certainly evident in the results of the informal opinion survey I undertook before starting this book. When asked about the current agenda for the field as indicated by published scholarship, a substantial majority of respondents insisted that much seems to be omitted. Research over time has grown less ambitious, they said, and increasingly pinched in scope – reflecting the timidity that I highlighted in Chapter 1. I am not alone in regarding that as one of the most serious failings of the field today. "We no longer ask big important questions," lamented one colleague; and the sentiment was echoed by many others using synonymous phrases like "broader issues," "fundamental problems," "old big questions," or "really big questions." Summarized one senior figure: "We can't predict the future, but the field could take more risks to explore some of the potentially existential challenges we could face in the next few years/decades." Among the mega-challenges that were said to demand more attention were climate change ("the big elephant in the room," according to one respondent), the rise of China, populism, nationalism, inequality, migration, and financialization. The wish list, all in all, was long and unambiguously ambitious.

Or consider all the "blind spots" addressed by the 2019 workshop at the Sheffield Political Economy Research Institute (SPERI) on "Political Economy on Trial," previously cited in Chapter 1. The whole point of the SPERI event was to illuminate gaps in the coverage of IPE research today. In the words of the workshop's organizers: "When we first hatched the event, we were driven by a suspicion that key dimensions of the world we live in continued to remain at the margins of IPE inquiry, even though they deserved to be far more central" (LeBaron et al. 2021: 284). Their purpose, they declared, was "to push the topics covered here higher up our scholarly agenda" (LeBaron et al. 2021: 284). Some of the gaps replicated the "big problems" highlighted in responses to my survey. Others roamed further afield to encompass essential matters of identity and culture – controversial social issues such as class, ethnicity, racism, gender, and coloniality.

The list could go on and on. What about cyber security, artificial intelligence, and other manifestations of the technology revolution that we are still living through? What about demography? Pandemics? Water shortages? Growing corporate concentration? The spread of nuclear weapons? Religious terrorism? And so on. It is not difficult to keep coming up with new problems to worry about. That's life. (A favorite definition of mine is: life is what happens when you have other plans.) The challenge is to know where to draw the line.

OUTER LIMITS

Despite the frequency of boundary battles, few attempts have been made to think in truly systematic fashion about the outer limits of IPE's agenda. There is no doubt about the practical importance of the many "big problems" and "blind spots" that are said to warrant attention. Most suggestions, however, seem arbitrary, even random. Absent is much sense of priority. An apt example was provided a decade ago by Robert Keohane (2011), who listed five "big changes" that he felt warranted more attention than they had yet received. These mega-challenges were the spread of economic development, the rise of China, volatility in financial and energy markets, the growing importance of truly global actors, and the emergence of electronic technologies. But how were we to establish precedence? Where were we to begin? Keohane didn't say.

Arguably, we could go back to the modern field's origins. The core of today's IPE, it seems safe to assume, is rooted in the field's twin forebears, the disciplines of political science and economics. If IPE is about anything, it is about Robert Gilpin's "pursuit of power" and "pursuit of wealth" – issues of politics and governance as stressed by political scientists, along with matters relating to material welfare as emphasized by economists. That much should not be controversial. As I have said before, these may be regarded as the common denominator of our area of inquiry. But that still leaves much to consider. The question remains: From the field's long and ambitious wish list extending beyond that core, what else might reasonably be added?

A notable (and rare) effort to address this question can be found in the double special issue that followed the 2019 SPERI workshop, where the editors offer a three-way taxonomy of "blind spots": issues that should be on IPE's agenda but are not (Best et al. 2021; LeBaron et al. 2021).

Three causes of blindness are distinguished. There are *conceptual* blind spots, *empirical* blind spots, and *disciplinary* blind spots. Conceptual blind spots "occur when our analytical lenses lead us to view the objects of our studies in particular ways – in the process obscuring other possible ways of seeing and making sense of the world" (Best et al. 2021: 218). Empirical blind spots "involve either ignoring or treating as peripheral problems and processes that are in fact central" (Best et al. 2021: 218). Disciplinary blind spots are practices "in and through which we come to define the appropriate domain of political economic study, and the debates that define it, in overly narrow terms" (Best et al. 2021: 218).

Unfortunately, while valiant, the effort fails to help us very much. Despite careful phrasing, the three categories overlap substantially, blurring the lines between them. How much difference is there, for instance, between "obscuring other possible ways of seeing" (conceptual blind spots) and "ignoring or treating as peripheral" (empirical blind spots)? Or what separates "viewing the objects of our studies in particular ways" (conceptual blind spots) from "defining the appropriate domain of political economic studies" (disciplinary blind spots)? And these overlaps in turn make it difficult to know how to label any of the many substantive issues on the field's wish list. Is IPE's widely deplored reluctance to address "really big questions" due to definitions of the field's domain that are framed "in overly narrow terms" (disciplinary blind spots)? Or is it caused by a tendency to "treat as peripheral problems ... that are in fact central" (empirical blind spots)? Is the relative paucity of work on the "big elephant" of climate change to be considered an empirical blind spot (treating as peripheral a problem that is in fact central) or a disciplinary blind spot (defining the domain of study in overly narrow terms)? It is noteworthy that after the taxonomy is formally introduced by the editors, little use is actually made of it in the discussions that follow.

A more fruitful approach would focus not on the causes for blindness but rather on what, if anything, we can gain by widening our vision, adding yet more topics to our agenda. To avert yet more boundary battles, the appropriate criterion should be utility: What can we learn? Pick any issue on the field's extensive and ever-expanding wish list. Is there reason to believe that IPE can offer an insightful path into the topic? Can we realistically expect to learn something that is neither trivial nor obvious? There is no reason to believe that all of the problems of the real world are equally amenable to analysis through an IPE lens.

In actuality, topics can be expected to differ significantly in how naturally they fit within the parameters of the field. Some issues may best be addressed by other specialties or disciplines. Lines should be drawn accordingly. That does not mean setting boundaries that are tight and impermeable. In a dynamic and ever-changing world, that could lead eventually to atrophy, leaving the field increasingly out of touch with what really matters. Rather, it means that we should be flexible and pragmatic in electing what to study. Nothing should be rejected *a priori*. Priority, however, should be given to topics that seem most tractable within the broad contours of the discipline.

COMPARATIVE ADVANTAGE

At issue is what economists mean by the notion of *comparative advantage* – a concept that has been central to mainstream theories of international trade ever since it was first formally articulated by David Ricardo in the early nineteenth century. Earlier commentaries on trade, including Adam Smith's *Wealth of Nations*, had assumed that a nation would naturally export goods that it could produce at lower cost than anyone else. In other words, its exports would enjoy an *absolute* advantage over all possible rivals. But that was incorrect, Ricardo wrote. The proper comparison, he insisted, is not between prices for the same product in different countries (absolute advantage). The comparison should be between price *structures* in different countries – relative costs in one country as compared with relative costs in another (comparative advantage). Two nations might each produce wine more cheaply than cloth (the two commodities that Ricardo chose to use to illustrate his argument). But if one can produce wine three times as cheaply as cloth while the other produces wine only twice as cheaply as cloth, both will gain if the first concentrates on exporting wine while the second exports cloth. The first is said to have a comparative advantage in wine while the second has a comparative advantage in cloth. Overall, according to conventional theory, material value ("utility" in the language of economists) will be maximized through exchange.

Many students – particularly those with little prior training in formal economics – have a hard time comprehending comparative advantage. It is not exactly an intuitive concept. As an instructor, it took me many years to find a concise way to capture its logic. Raised speaking English, I had always naively assumed that there were just three levels of description available: normative, comparative, and superlative (e.g., good/ better/best). But then I discovered that in some other languages there are not three but four levels: not just good/better/best but good/better/*more better*/best. "Better" is absolute advantage. "More better" is comparative advantage. If two countries are both better at producing wine than cloth, the one that is *more* better will have a comparative advantage in wine. The one that is less better at wine, conversely, will be more better at cloth and thus has a comparative advantage in cloth. If the notion of comparative advantage is understood correctly, it is easy to grasp the humor of a meme that circulated across the internet a few years back celebrating the skills of a popular economist named Daron Acemoglu, a Turkish-born Armenian American who teaches at the Massachusetts Institute of Technology in the United States. According to the meme, which was created by one of his fans, "Daron Acemoglu's comparative advantage is that he is better at everything." The joke is that it should have read *absolute* advantage. Comparative advantage, by definition, allows that while you may be more better at some things, others will be more better at other things. You can't be more better at everything.

Applied to the What question in IPE, the notion of comparative advantage provides us with a convenient way to frame discussion. The strengths of the modern field of IPE are undeniable, as I emphasized in Chapter 1. But that does not mean that our field can do everything. IPE is not Daron Acemoglu. The challenge is to find what is or is not in the field's comparative advantage.

IMPLICATIONS

Unfortunately, the comparative advantage of a field of study cannot be easily measured. Unlike international trade, where the costs of producing wine or cloth (or any other commodity) can in principle be quantified with some degree of precision, the marginal value of adding another issue to IPE's agenda is ultimately a matter of subjective judgment – an educated "guesstimate" at best, an untutored stab in the dark at worst. In the social sciences, where replication of controlled experiments is rarely possible, there are no commonly agreed metrics that can be used for comparative purposes. Hence differences of opinion are endemic. What one theorist regards as central, another might see as peripheral. Where one perceives value added, another might judge little more than a monumental waste of time.

From this observation emerge three important implications. First, it becomes clear that the limits to IPE's agenda must be regarded as elastic. There is no fixed and impenetrable fence dividing the relevant from the irrelevant, the wheat from the chaff. Once again, Susan Strange's image of an "open range" comes to mind. No conception of the admissible should take priority simply because it got there first. Nor should any subject be automatically rejected merely because it has yet to demonstrate how it might relate to existing perspectives. Comparative advantage must be thought of as dynamic – not static but mutable. What seems out of bounds today might come to seem central tomorrow.

Second, it also becomes clear that differences of opinion about IPE's agenda cannot be regarded as random. In fact, they tend to be a direct reflection of the rich diversity that is such a prominent feature of the field. There is an old dictum in industrial design, attributed to the late nineteenth-century architect Louis Sullivan, that "form follows function." In our context it could be rephrased as "agenda follows attributes," referring to the characteristics that I introduced back in Chapter 2 to paint a Big Picture of IPE. Our idea of what issues are most salient inevitably derives from our choices of ontology, purpose, boundaries, and epistemology – in other words, from our responses to the Why and How questions. Each paradigm assumes a certain purpose and a certain analytical approach. Scholars who share a perspective in common are likely also to concur on *what* should be studied: the What question. Within the field's separate "networks and niches" we can expect to find in each a fairly high degree of group consensus on what ought to take precedence on the research agenda.

Finally, it is clear that no one wish list will fit all. That is the key point if we are to succeed in averting wasteful boundary battles. To seek out a single agenda for the field as a whole is, in fact, a fool's errand. Precisely because each discourse coalition can be expected to have its own singular consensus, differences among priorities seem unavoidable. It is hardly likely that all factions of the invisible college will find themselves gravitating toward precisely the same wish list. It is more realistic to accept that we will end up with multiple lists, each one the unique product of a different scholarly tradition. The diversity of IPE's many perspectives naturally gives rise to a variety of possible agendas. The comparative advantage of each school of thought needs to be assessed individually.

To illustrate, we can return briefly to the "big important questions" whose absence was lamented by so many of the respondents to my informal survey. Many "really big questions," in one way or another, involve the challenge of systemic transformation. There seems little doubt that some versions of heterodox theory – particularly system-level perspectives – are better equipped to address such questions than the more ahistorical approaches typical of IPE orthodoxy. Issues of change in the *longue durée*, calling for more general rather than partial-equilibrium analysis, are clearly in the comparative advantage of historical-relativist paradigms like world-systems theory or work inspired by Robert Cox. Historical evolution is their meat and drink. That does not mean that mainstream researchers must agree with everything – or, for that matter, anything – that more heterodox scholarship has to say on the subject. But it does suggest that they might have something to learn on such matters from their more radical counterparts. It clearly will be more difficult for mainstream scholars to make a truly convincing argument about systemic issues without paying at least some attention to what insights heterodox scholarship might be in a position to offer. Recall what I said in the previous chapter about David Lake's presidential address to the American Political Science Association (APSA). Orthodox approaches to the challenge of systemic transformation that ignore the contributions of more critical scholarship risk producing results that are thin at best.

Conversely, consider the edge that mainstream scholarship may enjoy when it comes to more partial-equilibrium analysis, addressing emerging policy issues like water shortages, cyber security, or corporate concentration. Here the Open Economy Politics (OEP) paradigm, with its fine-grained focus on decision making, offers a distinct advantage over many heterodox traditions that are concerned more with Critique than Comprehension. Just as heterodoxy can claim a comparative advantage over issues of change in the *longue durée*, orthodoxy earns points for its deeper exploration of behavior and processes in *l'histoire événementielle*.

ILLUSTRATIONS

Differences of comparative advantage among perspectives mean that separate agendas are likely to diverge considerably. How, then, do we establish priorities in the face of such a variety of wish lists?

Mini-reviews

In principle, one possibility might be simply to divide up responsibilities in some kind of Grand Design for the field as a whole. Big systemic questions could be conceded to heterodox scholars, for instance, while reserving micro- and mid-level policy issues for orthodoxy. But that would be unfortunate, akin to divorce. A formal division of labor could lead to irreversible rupture, breaking up the field altogether. In practice, our aim should not be to add to mutual animus between diverse factions of the invisible college. That would merely escalate the danger of inadvertent omission.

Rather, extending the argument of the previous chapter, our goal should be to do all we can to take advantage of the strengths of each separate approach. That begins with a simple acknowledgment. We must accept that within the broad expanse of IPE, comparative advantages can and do legitimately differ. In reality, every faction of the invisible college is likely to be "more better" at something; none of us is Daron Acemoglu. Hence priorities are likely to differ as well. The preferences of each intellectual tradition deserve to be respected, not rejected. There is nothing unnatural about the existence of a variety of possible agendas in a single field of study.

It follows, therefore, that we potentially have much to learn from each other. That does not mean that we should simply abandon our own research priorities in favor of someone else's. There is no reason to lose sight of our own comparative advantage. But it does mean that we could all be better off if we *pay more attention to what other schools are interested in.* What thoughts might have been overlooked? What insights might be gleaned? Respective agendas are a reflection of both the purposes favored by other intellectual traditions (the Why question) and the paradigms and perspectives that are adopted to pursue those goals (the How question). If we look more closely at topics that are prioritized by others, we might be able to enrich our own preferred line of study. We should search for force multiplication wherever we can find it.

In the following pages, I provide some illustrations of what all this might mean. Drawing on my own informal survey as well as from the SPERI double special issue, I have put together a representative sample of some half-dozen oft-mentioned "blind spots" – practical subjects that many scholars in the field seem to believe have not yet received the attention they deserve. The sample was assembled randomly. They do not necessarily represent my own preferences or priorities. They are meant simply to be illustrative of the elasticity of IPE's putative agendas.

The six topics in my sample are: (1) the rise of China; (2) climate change; (3) migration; (4) financialization; (5) gender; and (6) coloniality. These six divide broadly into three separate types:

> Type 1. The first two subjects (China, climate) are examples of "big important questions" that may be thought to lie near the traditional

core of IPE. These are issues that are dominated by economic and political considerations, closest to the historical roots of the field.

Type 2. The second two (migration, financialization) represent more specific challenges that extend beyond the core of IPE to overlap significantly with other related disciplines, such as sociology or history. These are issues that expand the meaning of "multidiscipline" beyond just the "pursuit of wealth" and the "pursuit of power."

Type 3. The final two (gender, coloniality) stretch horizons even further to encompass issues where economics and politics, as conventionally conceived, are mostly overshadowed by other social concerns. These last two subjects test the absolute limits of the field of IPE.

For each of the six topics, I again scanned all the articles published in the five years from 2015 to 2019 in *International Organization* (*IO*) and the *Review of International Political Economy* (*RIPE*), both previously examined for a different purpose in Chapter 3. In addition, I also included *International Studies Quarterly* (*ISQ*) and *New Political Economy* (*NPE*) to gain a broader picture. By general consensus, these four journals represent the top academic venues in the English language for cutting-edge scholarship in IPE (Seabrooke and Young 2017: 297).

Admittedly, even with the addition of *ISQ* and *NPE*, the picture remains incomplete. Much may yet be missed by not including books or more specialized "niche" journals as well. Clearly the four journals in my sample, on their own, cannot capture the full *breadth* of scholarship in the field today. Arguably, however, they do succeed in highlighting what is done at the *peak* of the field, the "commanding heights" where standards are set and ambitions defined. They clear the path for others to follow.

In each of the six cases in my sample I offer a sort of "mini-review" addressing the following questions:

1. What, if anything, has IPE had to say about the topic?
2. What factions within IPE seem to demonstrate a comparative advantage in addressing the topic?
3. What further value, if any, might be added by bringing in other IPE traditions?

The Rise of China

First in my sample is China. Half a century ago, the People's Republic of China (PRC) was an insignificant minnow in the ocean of the global economy. Today, after decades of record-breaking growth, the country has become a whale. By some measures China is now the world's single biggest national economy. A hegemonic transition would appear to be under way in global affairs, threatening the hitherto dominant position of the United States (US). Authoritarian China seems poised to reclaim its central position as the world's proverbial Middle Kingdom, shaking the foundations of the liberal international order. Keohane (2011) is by no means alone in listing the PRC's rise as one of the most important "big changes" in the world economy today. Many observers recall the prophetic words of the French emperor Napoleon Bonaparte, who declared "China is a sleeping giant. Let her sleep, for when she wakes she will move the world."

Not everyone sees China that way, of course. Some are more relaxed. Several years ago, for a meeting of the International Political Economy Society, I was invited to organize a panel discussion on what the PRC's ascent might mean for the study of IPE. During the question period that followed formal presentations, a senior colleague in the audience asked, in all seriousness, "Why can't we treat China as just one more data point?" The answer, it seemed to me, was obvious. Yes, it is possible that China represents just one more data point. That would mean that the country may be moving the world, but in degree only, not necessarily in kind. It is causing change *within* rather than transformation *of* the global system. But how can we be sure? The impact of the now-awakened giant cannot simply be assumed. That really would be an abdication of responsibility.

Significantly, many in IPE concur. Contrary to those who include China among the field's alleged "blind spots," there has actually been a flood of research on the country and its place in the global system – at least as evidenced by the four journals under review. In those venues during the five years from 2015 to 2019, no fewer than 68 articles were published that touched on the Middle Kingdom's re-emergence in one way or another, an average of more than one contribution per month. That hardly seems like neglect.

In most cases, however, the focus of analysis was relatively narrow. Of the 68 articles, just a handful directly addressed broad systemic implications of China's revival. That was especially evident in *IO*, the preferred home for more orthodox IPE research, where in the five years under review just eight papers related to the PRC in any way; and of those eight, most were tightly centered on selected problem areas such as trade disputes or intellectual property rights. The assumption seemed to be that

China is indeed just one more data point. The aim was Comprehension, not Critique and certainly not Counsel. Only one of the eight studies took on the broad issue of hegemonic transition directly – a thoughtful analysis in a constructivist vein of the role that identity might play in the evolution of the global order (Allan et al. 2018). Such a sharp skew is not particularly surprising given the ahistorical character of most mainstream IPE scholarship. As I have suggested, we would not expect orthodoxy to have a comparative advantage when it comes to the "really big question" of systemic transformation.

More surprising is the relative scarcity of more expansive analyses in the three other journals as well, even though all of them normally tend to be more hospitable than *IO* to heterodox work of various strains. Each of the publications carried two to three times as many China-related articles as did *IO*. Yet here too the vast majority were mostly in the vein of conventional micro- or mid-level theory, taking the broader global order as a given. Favorite topics included internationalization of the PRC's currency and related exchange-rate issues, global production networks, and Chinese overseas lending. The work is generally of high quality and often quite insightful, but not particularly daring. A rare exception came from T.V. Paul (2017), a Canadian-based scholar, when he was elected president of the International Studies Association. (Notably, his contribution came in the form of a presidential address, not a standard research paper.) In a challenging discussion, Paul disputed the commonly held view that hegemonic transitions such as we seem to be facing today can be expected, typically, to end in armed conflict. Peaceful change, he argued, is possible, but only if leading powers, including China especially, can be induced to reorient significantly their grand strategies in foreign policy. And a few other scholars explored the leadership role that the PRC might play in multilateral trade and development organizations (Hopewell 2015; Heldt and Schmidtke 2019; Stephen and Parizek 2019). In total, however, the exceptions were few and far between.

Viewed in terms of comparative advantage, therefore, it would seem that this record represents a massive opportunity foregone. The rise of China clearly is not being ignored in the leading journals; a flow of papers at a rate greater than one per month hardly qualifies as a blind spot. But the attention that is being paid is unmistakably skewed toward one or another of the three stages of the OEP paradigm. Some studies focus on interests, others on domestic institutions, and yet others on inter-state bargaining – all very much in the comparative advantage of familiar mainstream traditions. The comparative advantage of more heterodox approaches, by contrast, remains under-exploited. Where are the insights to be drawn from the historical-relativist paradigms of diverse system-level theories? Where is critical theory? Where is cultural IPE? To date, scholarship in the leading IPE journals appears content to draw the line on China modestly, largely excluding more general themes. That seems a major loss for the field.

Climate Change

Next comes the "big elephant in the room" – climate change. Half a century ago, how many of us worried about the global environment? Despite the warnings of a few dedicated climate scientists, mostly derided as cranks, we went about our daily lives heedlessly burning fossil fuels, discarding plastic products, and cutting down forests. Today, by contrast, the burden of proof is on those who would deny the reality of what looks like impending catastrophe. Temperatures are rising, glaciers are melting, and major weather events are becoming both more numerous and more extreme. Over the 4.5 billion years of the Earth's existence, there have been five mass extinctions on a global scale, all the result of natural causes. The most recent was 65 million years ago (just yesterday in geological time) when an asteroid impact ended up killing off the dinosaurs. Now the luminous "blue marble" that astronauts viewed with awe from the moon seems caught in the grip of a new geological epoch. We appear to face the danger of a sixth mass extinction, this time man-made. The era has been dubbed the Anthropocene.

Like the rise of China, the relevance of climate change to IPE seems obvious. The environment, after all, involves us all, functioning much like a public good. It is akin to the grassy common that featured at the center of old New England villages, owned by none and available to all for grazing or other purposes. Yet authority over the environment's use is fragmented and contested, leading to free-riding, excessive exploitation, and degradation – a classic collective-action problem. The "tragedy of the common" knows no borders; moreover, economic and political considerations are obviously central, encompassing a wide range of actors and institutions. It is hardly surprising, therefore, to find climate change on many wish lists for our field.

Here too, as in the case of China, research activity has been greater than many realize. In practice, the Anthropocene has proved to be not much more of a blind spot than has the rise of the PRC. Climate change too has attracted a fair degree of attention. During the years from 2015 to 2019, again as evidenced by the four journals under review, some 34 articles were published bearing in some way on the issue. That may not be quite the flood of work we saw on China, but neither can it be seen as a sign of serious neglect. If specialists in the field feel that the subject is under-researched, it may be because the lion's share of scholarship has appeared in just one journal, *NPE*, which is not widely read outside Britain. Of the 34 articles, 20 appeared in *NPE* (with eleven more that came out in *NPE* in 2020, just beyond my sample period). In *IO*, by contrast, there was just one climate-related article during the entire five-year period, and in *ISQ* and *RIPE* only a small handful of papers touching on the subject.

Unlike what we saw in the China case, however, a significant number of climate articles were much more in the vein of Critique than Comprehension. There were of course papers pitched in orthodox fashion at the level of familiar micro- or mid-level theory, demonstrating the comparative advantage of more mainstream approaches in dealing with partial-equilibrium analysis in *l'histoire événementielle*. Informative studies ran the gamut from the role of domestic and transnational interests in shaping climate policy (Genovese 2019; Kuzemko 2019) to the mechanisms by which environmental initiatives diffuse across space and time (Genovese et al. 2017). But in contrast to the China case, there were also many papers that clearly bore the imprint of heterodoxy. That the global climate is changing was taken as a given in these contributions. Their aim, in most instances, was to offer a critical interpretation of the transformations that are occurring today or are in prospect. One survey explored what different strands of historical materialist IPE might have to say about an anticipated transition to a low-carbon global economy (Newell 2019). Another addressed what are described as the "negative environmental contradictions of contemporary capitalism" (Farrell 2015). And yet others took up inherent ethical issues (Dirix 2015) or the "commodification of nature" (Richardson 2015). On the subject of climate change, heterodox scholars seem no more reluctant to build on their comparative advantage than do their more mainstream counterparts.

What is striking, however, is the deafening silence that persists between orthodox and heterodox contributions. Critical commentaries at the systemic level pay little attention to more orthodox studies of relevant interests or institutions; they rarely get down into the weeds of policymaking or international bargaining. Conversely, mainstream treatments cite few, if any, papers by more radical authors, preferring to remain firmly anchored instead in the formal literature they know best. The result, on both sides of the orthodox/heterodox divide, is the pathology of inadvertent omission – a reciprocal failure even to try to appreciate what other approaches might have to offer. Possibilities for force multiplication are generally ignored. That too may be regarded as an opportunity foregone.

Migration

The third topic in my sample is migration – the relocation of people across national frontiers. Flows of goods and services (otherwise known as trade) along with flows of money and capital (otherwise known as finance) have long figured at the heart of IPE. Trade is what the global economy is all about; finance is the lubricant that keeps the wheels of commerce humming. Movements of people, by contrast, have only recently begun to receive serious attention from scholars in the field. Many in IPE's invisible college believe that migration still ranks as one of the field's most conspicuous blind spots. One colleague in private correspondence declares that: migration "needs to be more firmly incorporated" into our analyses. Another describes it, charmingly, as the "most intimate form of globalization."

The subject's claim to importance is hard to deny. Overall, in recent years, more than 250 million persons on average have changed their country of residence annually – some 3.5 percent of the world's population each year. (If migrants were a single nation, they would rank fifth in the world, after China, India, the US, and Indonesia.) Some people move willingly for general reasons like better job opportunities or healthcare needs. Others are refugees and asylum seekers driven to take flight because of, *inter alia*, armed conflict, oppression, or high crime rates. Both economic and political factors are obviously involved. But so too are controversial social and cultural considerations that often dominate public discussion. As compared with Type 1 subjects like China or climate change, migration clearly takes us further away from the historical core of IPE. In my classification it is a Type 2 issue, not quite in the same class of undoubted "big questions." Some would question whether it warrants precedence on IPE's agenda.

Warranted or not, however, the topic has been gaining attention (Talani 2015). Indeed, much as in the cases of China and climate change, research activity on migration too has been greater than many realize. In the four journals in my mini-review during the years 2015–19, some 26 articles touched on the issue. That was almost as many as the number of papers addressing the big elephant of climate change. Greater distance from IPE's core has not discouraged considerable interest.

The pattern of interest seems similar to that for climate change. First, once again, relatively few studies appeared in *IO* – only five in total. All five, as might be expected, were cast at the level of conventional micro- or mid-level theory, relying heavily on formal empirical methodology. All played to the comparative advantage of the American style of IPE. One article examined linkages between migration and the allocation of foreign development assistance (Bermeo and Leblang 2015), while others took up topics like human trafficking (Simmons et al. 2018) or the conflict perceptions of migrants (Koubi et al. 2018). Perhaps most noteworthy was a well-crafted analysis by two US scholars, based on an interest-driven voting model, that dissected variations in the external labor openness of major destination countries (Bearce and Hart 2017). None of the *IO* articles chose to stand back to consider broader systemic effects of migration.

Second, here too, articles in the other three journals included a significant number of papers that were more in the vein of Critique than Comprehension. One examined the "commodification of citizenship" that may be regarded as part of a "neoliberal political economy of belonging" (Mavelli 2018). Another highlighted the "capitalist value regimes" that drive migrants to struggle "to translate their body power into valorised labor" (Rajaram 2018: 627). And a third explored how national immigration policies affect the "problem of contemporary free labor" (LeBaron and Phillips 2019). Work like this clearly demonstrates the comparative advantage of more critical scholarship. Arguably, considerable value may be added by challenging the ingrained perspectives of more orthodox schools of thought.

And third, as in the climate case, we find a deafening silence between mainstream and more radical contributions – yet again, the pathology of inadvertent omission. If migration is believed to be one of IPE's blind spots, it is, at least in part, because scholars on both sides regrettably have chosen to remain largely myopic on the subject: another opportunity foregone.

Financialization

Fourth in my sample is financialization, also known as assetization. This topic too may be classified as a Type 2 issue. As commonly understood, financialization refers to the ever-expanding role of capital markets, debt, and financial services in the modern world (Epstein 2005). Finance of course has long played a role in heterodox analyses of global capitalism. The earliest full-fledged theory of economic imperialism, dating back to the first decade of the twentieth century, placed finance squarely at center stage. The theory came from the pen of the Englishman John A. Hobson, a radical liberal journalist (not to be confused with his grandson John M. Hobson, a contemporary academic previously cited in Chapter 2). In John A. Hobson's words: "By far the most important economic factor in Imperialism is the influence relating to investments" (Hobson 1902: 51). Struggle over the disposition of surplus capital, he said, was the "taproot" of imperialism. And that theme in turn was soon seized upon by disciples of Karl Marx, including most prominently the Austrian Rudolf Hilferding and, of course, the Russian V.I. Lenin in his *Imperialism: The Highest Stage of Capitalism.*

Generations later, the role of transnational finance seems to many to be greater than ever. As a colleague of mine wrote to me, IPE needs to "really go 'hard' on the remarkable transformation of global finance, its complexity, how transnational finance capital is now at the very core of the world economy ... This focus should be at the heart of a renewed IPE." Many others in the field concur. Prominent contributors include Anastasia Nesvetailova (2011), a British-based scholar, and the team of Jeffrey Chwieroth, also based in London, and Andrew Walter, an Australian (Chwieroth and Walter 2019).

Interestingly, however, the overwhelming majority of work on finan-cialization in my sample of journals – as was true in the case of climate change – has been concentrated in just one publication: *NPE*. In all, some 30 papers were published in the four journals under review during the years from 2015 to 2019. All but four were in *NPE*. Not a single article relating to financialization appeared in either *IO* or *ISQ*. In those two journals, the subject was most conspicuous by its absence. It is as if for more mainstream scholars, who are most represented in *IO* and *ISQ*, the issue did not even exist. This was more than myopia; this was absolute blindness.

For more heterodox sources, by contrast, financialization not only exists – as represented by the flock of articles in *NPE* – it is seen as a matter of utmost importance. Many of the papers in *NPE* sought to critique the role of finance in modern society, reflecting the comparative advantage of critical theories of various stripes. An outstanding example was provided by Nesvetailova in a detailed analysis of the structural role of shadow banking in contemporary capitalism (Nesvetailova 2015).

Sylvia Maxfield, an American, and colleagues dissected evidence for claims of global homogenization toward a singular model of finance capitalism – an idea known as the "financialization convergence hypothesis" (Maxfield et al. 2017). And others explored such matters as the "material cultures" of financialization (Bayliss et al. 2017) or the nature of "capitalist money" (Barredo-Zuriarrain 2019). There appears to be little blindness to the issue here.

In effect, what we see is something of a mirror image of the pattern of scholarship that we observed in the China case. There we found a sharp skew toward more conventional micro- or mid-level theory, with heterodox approaches under-exploited. In this case we find the reverse – a sharp tilt in favor of more radical or critical theory, with orthodox approaches under-represented. Discussion of financialization, for the most part, is confined to just one side of the orthodox/heterodox divide, with hardly a word from the other side. That too can be seen as an opportunity foregone.

Gender

Gender, fifth in my sample, takes us even further from the traditional core of IPE. In the eyes of a good number of scholars – men and women alike – feminism represents a glaring void in the field. As noted back in Chapter 2, conventional perspectives in IPE are criticized for implicitly favoring masculine interpretations of different kinds of economic activity. Serious biases thus run through the field that tend to work to the disadvantage of women. That is particularly true of what is called "social reproduction" – the non-market (i.e., unpaid) work needed to create a home life, provide leisure activities, and care for family members. These activities are almost universally associated with feminine characteristics and thus tend to be assigned mostly to women. For years, eminent scholars like V. Spike Peterson (2018) in the US, Isabella Bakker (2007) in Canada, Juanita Elias (2011) in Britain, and Penny Griffin (2007) in Australia have campaigned to extend the boundaries of IPE to incorporate the vital role of the reproductive economy. Deep analysis of the implications of gendered hierarchies, they argue, would provide a fuller understanding of behavior in global economic affairs. In the words of one recent commentary: "The inclusion of gender as a central concept within IPE ... would radically transform [our] understanding of the field's basic subject matter" (Clift et al. 2021).

In practice, however, despite prodigious efforts, pleas for a feminist IPE have fallen largely on deaf ears. As compared with headline issues like China, climate, or migration, gender has gained relatively little traction in the field. In the words of one frustrated source, "both mainstream and critical IPE scholars [find] it easy to ignore and/or sideline the contributions of feminist work ... feminist scholarship has been rendered invisible" (Elias and Roberts 2018: 1). That certainly seems confirmed by my own brief mini-review. During 2015–19 no more than nine gender-related papers appeared in the four journals in my sample. *IO* once again trailed the field, without a single contribution. The other three publications averaged a total of three articles each, a rate of less than one paper a year. The reason for the paucity of output is unclear. It could be because gender-related work has difficulty clearing the traditional peer-review processes of the leading journals; or it may be because feminist scholars prefer to submit their work to other more specialized outlets where they can hope to find a more receptive audience. Either way, the evidence clearly suggests a major opportunity foregone.

As might be expected, given feminist IPE's outsider status, few of the nine papers that made it into print could be classified as orthodox in style. A rare exception was a well-conceived micro-level study of gender's effect on trade preferences by Edward Mansfield, a noted veteran of the American school, and two colleagues (Mansfield et al. 2015). Most of the other articles were much more heterodox in tone, more concerned with Critique than Comprehension. Several self-identified as "critical feminist political economy" (Hozić and True 2017; Roberts and Zulfiqar 2019), while others explicitly targeted neoliberal capitalism and the "neoliberalization of feminism" (Pruegl 2015; Ferragina 2019). Radical approaches are bound to have a comparative advantage in addressing a subject that has not yet been widely accepted as a legitimate part of the field's agenda.

Coloniality

Finally we come to coloniality, an even less widely accepted – or understood – topic. The "coloniality of power" is an expression first coined just two decades ago by Anibal Quijano (2000), a Peruvian sociologist. It refers to structures of implicit social control, born during the age of colonialism, that are said to persist down to the present day, even after formal decolonization. At issue are systems of cultural, political, and economic hierarchy that allegedly prioritize Western values at the expense of more peripheral nations and regions. Bright Eurocentric notions of modernity, progress, and development, it is argued, cannot be separated from the more pernicious practices of imperialism, enslavement, and racism. They are, as it were, two sides of the same coin. In the words of one recent commentary: "Coloniality then constitutes modernity's festering violent underbelly, its 'dark side,' and describes all those colonial systems of oppression and exploitation that have survived formal 'decolonization'" (Mantz 2019: 1363).

In recent years the issue of coloniality has been gaining considerable attention in academic circles, particularly in Europe and Latin America. In some places it has even led to a lively movement to "decolonize the university" (Bhambra et al. 2018) or, at a minimum, to "decolonize the curriculum" (Muldoon 2019). Specifically in IPE, however, the impact to date has been minimal. As with gender (and most likely for the same reasons), the issue has so far failed to gain much traction, at least as suggested by the four journals under review. During the 2015–19 period there were just six articles that touched on coloniality in any way. Once again *IO* trailed the field with not a single paper relating to the issue. Readers of *IO* can hardly be blamed if they admit they have never even heard of the notion of coloniality. Like financialization and gender, this is a topic that seems to attract discussion mostly on just one side of the orthodox/heterodox divide. Contributions are overwhelmingly critical in style, addressing such matters as the presumed colonial and racial origins of the welfare state (Bhambra 2018) or the biases of Western-dominated trade analysis (Scott 2015). Here too we see how much comparative advantage more radical approaches may enjoy when a subject has yet to gain a firm perch on IPE's agenda.

Patterns

As indicated, the half-dozen topics in my sample can be understood to be representative of the three major types of issue that tend to appear on IPE wish lists. When they were chosen, I had no preconceptions about what to expect; nor, as noted, was I unaware of the risk of limiting analysis to just the four leading journals in the field. Yet the results, it turns out, are striking. Certain distinct regularities clearly do emerge that might help us in rethinking the What question more generally. Four patterns stand out.

First, there are unmistakable differences in the amount of attention paid to each of the three types of "blind spots." A strong positive relationship exists between an issue's proximity to the field's core and the number of studies devoted to it. In all, some 173 articles relating to the six topics were found in the four journals under review during the years 2015–19. That seems to suggest that in the aggregate the sample subjects were not in fact truly neglected. But of that total, almost 60 percent (102) were accounted for by the two Type 1 issues alone. Type 2 topics, by contrast, accounted for just one-third (56) and Type 3 subjects for less than 10 percent (15). It appears that the more an issue appears to diverge from the traditional "P" and "E" of IPE, the less inclined many scholars are to seriously engage with it. Or, to put the point more succinctly (and bluntly): the less familiar the topic, the lower the level of research activity. That seems to be a safe generalization.

Second, there are also unmistakable differences in the scale of attention paid to our sample subjects by each of the four journals, which suggests in turn corresponding differences among IPE's diverse schools of thought. At one extreme is *IO*, the favorite of more mainstream scholarship. *IO* showed the least enthusiasm for unfamiliar topics of any kind. That was true for every one of the six "blind spots" that were examined. Only 14 related papers were published in the journal, amounting to little more than 8 percent of the five-year total. For half the topics, there was not a single entrant in *IO*. At the opposite extreme was *NPE*, the journal most amenable to more heterodox perspectives, with some 75 papers representing almost 45 percent of the total. Earlier I noted that timidity may be considered to be one of the most serious pathologies in IPE today. The evidence here suggests that, by and large, heterodox scholars are less inhibited in their ambition than their more orthodox counterparts. They appear more willing, in practice, to think outside the box. That too seems to be a safe generalization. The very definition of heterodoxy, after all, is to challenge orthodoxy. It is no accident that many on the heterodox side of the field self-define as "radical."

Third, there are some major opportunities foregone that remain under-exploited. One example is the China case, where heterodox scholars have yet to make much use of their comparative advantage in system-level analysis. Other examples include our Type 2 and Type 3 topics, where we see a striking paucity of the sort of systematic micro- or mid-level explorations that play to the strengths of more orthodox approaches. There appears to be ample room to add value in the study of all these diverse issues.

Finally, there is in most cases a thick wall of silence between the two sides of the orthodox/heterodox divide. Little effort on either side goes into considering seriously what the other side has to say. Instead, the widespread prevalence of inadvertent omission and overt opposition is confirmed. Only rarely do we find systematic attempts to make use of the field's pluralism as a force multiplier. Even more rare are efforts to go "beyond paradigms" to search for hidden commonalities and connections among competing perspectives. It is clear that more could be done to encourage the field's diverse cohorts to learn more from one another.

CONCLUSION

The aim of this chapter has been to rethink the agenda for research in IPE. Can more boundary battles be averted? Researchers have no difficulty in coming up with more and more topics that might be considered "blind spots" in the field: substantive issues that have yet to receive the attention they are thought to deserve. Upon reflection, however, it seems evident that limits to IPE's agenda are bound to be elastic. Ideas about what should take precedence can be expected to vary from one faction to another, depending on how each positions itself on the Why and How questions. A review of some half-dozen alleged gaps in the field illustrates how much value could be added to analysis if more attention is paid to what other discourse coalitions prioritize. Again, as in Chapters 3 and 4, much depends on the practicalities of implementation. That all-important matter will be taken up next.

REFERENCES

Allan, Bentley B., Srdjan Vucetik, and Ted Hopf (2018), "The Distribution of Identity and the Future of International Order: China's Hegemonic Prospects," *International Organization* 72:4, 839–69.

Bakker, Isabella (2007), "Social Reproduction and the Constitution of a Gendered Political Economy," *New Political Economy* 12:4, 541–56.

Barredo-Zuriarrain, Juan (2019), "The Nature of Capitalist Money and the Financial Links Between Debt-Led and Export-Led Growth Regimes," *New Political Economy* 24:4, 565–86.

Bayliss, Kate, Ben Fine, and Mary Robertson (2017), "Introduction to a Special Issue on the Material Cultures of Financialization," *New Political Economy*, 22:4, 355–70.

Bearce, David H. and Andrew F. Hart (2017), "International Labor Mobility and the Variety of Democratic Political Institutions," *International Organization* 71:1, 65–95.

Bermeo, Sarah B. and David Leblang (2015), "Migration and Foreign Aid," *International Organization* 69:3, 627–57.

Best, Jacqueline, Colin Hay, Genevieve LeBaron, and Daniel Mügge (2021), "Seeing and Not-seeing Like a Political Economist: The Historicity of

Contemporary Political Economy and its Blind Spots," *New Political Economy* 26:2, 217–28.

Bhambra, Gurminder K. (2018), "Colonialism, Postcolonialism and the Liberal Welfare State," *New Political Economy* 23:5, 574–87.

Bhambra, Gurminder K., Dalia Gebrial, and Kerem Nişancioğlu, eds. (2018), *Decolonising the University* (London: Pluto Press).

Chwieroth, Jeffrey M. and Andrew Walter (2019), *The Wealth Effect: How the Great Expectations of the Middle Class Have Changed the Politics of Banking Crises* (New York: Cambridge University Press).

Clift, Ben, Peter M. Kristensen, and Ben Rosamond (2021), "Remembering and Forgetting IPE: Disciplinary History as Boundary Work," *Review of International Political Economy* (forthcoming).

Dirix, Jo (2015), "Is the EU ETS a Just Climate Policy?" *New Political Economy* 20:5, 702–24.

Elias, Juanita (2011), "Critical Feminist Scholarship and IPE," in Stuart Shields, Ian Bruff, and Huw Macartney, eds., *Critical International Political Economy: Dialogue, Debate and Dissensus* (Basingstoke, UK: Palgrave Macmillan), 99–116.

Elias, Juanita and Adrienne Roberts (2018), "Introduction: Situating Gender Scholarship in IPE," in Juanita Elias and Adrienne Roberts, eds., *Handbook on the International Political Economy of Gender* (Cheltenham, UK and Northampton, MA, USA: Edward Elgar Publishing), 1–20.

Epstein, Gerald A., ed. (2005), *Financialization and the World Economy* (Cheltenham, UK and Northampton, MA, USA: Edward Elgar Publishing).

Farrell, Nathan (2015), "Multilateral Organizations and the Limits to International Energy Cooperation," *New Political Economy* 20:1, 85–106.

Ferragina, Emanuele (2019), "The Political Economy of Family Policy Expansion: Fostering Neoliberal Capitalism or Promoting Gender Equality Supporting Social Reproduction?" *Review of International Political Economy* 26:6, 1238–65.

Genovese, Federica (2019), "Sectors, Pollution, and Trade: How Industrial Interests Shape Domestic Positions on Global Climate Agreements," *International Studies Quarterly* 63:4, 819–36.

Genovese, Federica, Florian G. Kern, and Christian Martin (2017), "Policy Alteration: Rethinking Diffusion Processes When Policies Have Alternatives," *International Studies Quarterly* 61:2, 236–52.

Griffin, Penny (2007), "Refashioning IPE: What and How Gender Analysis Teaches International (Global) Political Economy," *Review of International Political Economy* 14:4, 719–36.

Heldt, Eugénia and Henning Schmidtke (2019), "Explaining Coherence in International Regime Complexes: How the World Bank Shapes the Field of Multilateral Development Finance," *Review of International Political Economy* 26:6, 1160–86.

Hobson, John A. (1902), *Imperialism: A Study* (New York: James Pott and Company).

Hopewell, Kristen (2015), "Different Paths to Power: The Rise of Brazil, India, and China at the World Trade Organization," *Review of International Political Economy* 22:2, 311–38.

Hozić, Aida A. and Jacqui True (2017), "Brexit as a Scandal: Gender and Global Trumpism," *Review of International Political Economy* 24:2, 270–87.

Keohane, Robert O. (2011), "The Old IPE and the New," in Nicola Phillips and Catherine E. Weaver, eds., *International Political Economy: Debating the Past, Present and Future* (London: Routledge), 35–44.

Koubi, Vally, Tobias Böhmelt, Gabriele Spilker, and Lena Schaffer (2018), "The Determinants of Environmental Migrants' Conflict Perception," *International Organization* 72:4, 905–36.

Kuzemko, Caroline (2019), "Re-Scaling IPE: Local Governments, Sustainable Energy and Change," *Review of International Political Economy* 26:1, 80–103.

LeBaron, Genevieve and Nicola Phillips (2019), "States and the Political Economy of Unfree Labour," *New Political Economy* 24:1, 1–21.

LeBaron, Genevieve, Daniel Mügge, Jacqueline Best, and Colin Hay (2021), "Blind Spots in IPE: Marginalized Perspectives and Neglected Trends in Contemporary Capitalism," *Review of International Political Economy* 28:2, 283–94.

Mansfield, Edward, Diana C. Mutz, and Laura R. Silver (2015), "Men, Women, Trade, and Free Markets," *International Studies Quarterly* 59:2, 303–15.

Mantz, Felix (2019), "Decolonizing the IPE Syllabus: Eurocentrism and the Coloniality of Knowledge in International Political Economy," *Review of International Political Economy* 26:6, 1361–78.

Mavelli, Luca (2018), "Citizenship for Sale and the Neoliberal Political Economy of Belonging," *International Studies Quarterly* 62:3, 482–93.

Maxfield, Sylvia, W. Kindred Winecoff, and Kevin L. Young (2017), "An Empirical Investigation of the Financialization Convergence Hypothesis," *New Political Economy* 24:6, 1004–29.

Muldoon, James (2019), "Academics: It's Time to Get Behind Decolonising the Curriculum," *The Guardian*, March 20.

Nesvetailova, Anastasia (2011), *Financial Alchemy in Crisis: The Great Liquidity Illusion* (London: Pluto Press).

Nesvetailova, Anastasia (2015), "A Crisis of the Overcrowded Future: Shadow Banking and the Political Economy of Financial Innovation," *New Political Economy* 20:3, 431–53.

Newell, Peter (2019), "Transformismo or Transformation? The Global Political Economy of Energy Transitions," *Review of International Political Economy* 26:1, 25–48.

Paul, T.V. (2017), "Recasting Statecraft: International Relations and Strategies of Peaceful Change," *International Studies Quarterly* 61:1, 1–13.

Peterson, V. Spike (2018), "Problematic Premises: Positivism, Modernism and Masculinism in IPE," in Juanita Elias and Adrienne Roberts, eds., *Handbook on the International Political Economy of Gender* (Cheltenham, UK and Northampton, MA, USA: Edward Elgar Publishing), 23–36.

Pruegl, Elisabeth (2015), "Neoliberalising Feminism," *New Political Economy* 20:4, 614–31.

Quijano, Anibal (2000), "Coloniality of Power and Eurocentrism in Latin America," *International Sociology* 15:2, 215–32.

Rajaram, Prem K. (2018), "Refugees as Surplus Population: Race, Migration and Capitalist Value Regimes," *New Political Economy* 23:5, 627–39.

Richardson, Ben (2015), "Making a Market for Sustainability: The Commodification of Certified Palm Oil," *New Political Economy* 20:4, 545–68.

Roberts, Adrienne and Ghazal Mir Zulfiqar (2019), "The Political Economy of Women's Entrepreneurship Initiatives in Pakistan: Reflections on Gender, Class, and 'Development,'" *Review of International Political Economy* 26:3, 410–35.

Scott, James (2015), "The Role of Southern Intellectuals in Contemporary Trade Governance," *New Political Economy* 20:5, 633–52.

Seabrooke, Leonard and Kevin L. Young (2017), "The Networks and Niches of International Political Economy," *Review of International Political Economy* 24:2, 288–331.

Simmons, Beth A., Paulette Lloyd, and Brandon M. Stewart (2018), "The Global Diffusion of Law: Transnational Crime and the Case of Human Trafficking," *International Organization* 72:2, 249–81.

Stephen, Matthew D. and Michal Parizek (2019), "New Powers and the Distribution of Preferences in Global Trade Governance: From Deadlock and Drift to Fragmentation," *New Political Economy* 24:6, 735–58.

Talani, Leila S. (2015), "International Migration: IPE Perspectives and the Impact of Globalisation," in Leila S. Talani and Simon McMahon, eds., *Handbook of the International Political Economy of Migration* (Cheltenham, UK and Northampton, MA, USA: Edward Elgar Publishing), 17–36.

6. The Big Challenge

The pathologies besetting International Political Economy (IPE) are plain to see. Our once-vibrant field of study has indeed drifted unhealthily off-track, raising critical – even existential – questions about its future well-being. There is ample room for worry. What is the purpose of the field (the Why question)? What can or should be done about paradigmatic diversity in the field (the How question)? What practical issues should be addressed in the field (the What question)? IPE's invisible college has come to be deeply divided over all three questions. The problem is to know what to do about them.

Can IPE get its groove back? Can vitality be restored? In principle, numerous remedies are available that might help rehabilitate the field. But good intentions are not enough. How can we ensure that prescriptions will actually be adopted? That is where the practicalities of implementation come in. Realistically, some degree of resistance to change must be expected. It is not easy to alter minds that have long been made up. Hence prescriptions must come with a set of instructions. Lofty new goals, on their own, will not suffice no matter how attractive they may seem. We must also think seriously about *strategy* – how to overcome stubborn forces of inertia to achieve desired objectives. In simplest terms, we need a plan of action to get us from Here to There. That is our Big Challenge. Three steps are required.

HERE AND THERE

The first step is to be clear about both Here and There. Where are we today, and where do we want to go?

Here

In IPE today, "Here" is defined by the Why, How, and What questions. Each of these core questions has been explored in a preceding chapter. Discussion has directed attention to five key pathologies that call out for remedy.

The Why question is about the purpose of our field of inquiry. Why do we study IPE? Three possibilities were discussed in Chapter 3: Comprehension (positivist explanation), Critique (normative criticism), and Counsel (policy engagement). Of these three, Counsel tends to be the least favored option by far, while open hostility prevails between advocates of Comprehension or Critique. This skewed mix generates a pair of dangerous pathologies for the field as a whole, which I labeled "unilateral disdain" and "mutual animus." Unilateral disdain discourages policy-oriented research and risks seeing the field condemned to irrelevance. Mutual animus pits orthodoxy against heterodoxy and could lead to irreversible fragmentation of the field.

The How question is about the diversity of our field of study. How should we study IPE? The field today incorporates a remarkably wide range of paradigms and research traditions, together producing a robust intellectual ecology. But too much of the time IPE's diverse approaches have gotten segregated into separate silos that become effectively insular if not wholly isolated from one another. The overall result is balkanization – a sense of scattered disarray, even chaos. That exposes the field to another pair of dangerous pathologies, which I called "inadvertent omission" and "overt opposition." Inadvertent omission refers to the myopic parochialism that afflicts many factions of the invisible college, owing to their limited familiarity with the full range of available theoretical approaches. Overt opposition describes the possibility that other perspectives may be familiar but are actively rejected, threatening animus and perhaps even paradigm war. Here too the ultimate outcome could be fatal fragmentation.

Finally, the What question is about the agenda for research in IPE. What issues should be addressed in the field? The What question gives rise to yet one more grievous pathology – "boundary battles." While many IPE scholars are content with a docket narrowly confined to the core of the field, with parameters derived solely from the disciplines of political science and economics, others seek to extend coverage more broadly to all kinds of other supposed "blind spots." In reality, Chapter 5 contended, the limits to IPE's agenda are bound to be elastic, reflecting the varied interests of diverse cohorts. Each faction of the invisible college is apt to have its own comparative advantage in material applications. Hence the diversity of the field must be expected to give rise to a variety of possible agendas. Yet, sadly, endless disputes tend to arise over where to draw the line, exacerbating tensions already provoked by the Why and How questions. Debates over purpose and paradigms become fights about alleged substantive gaps in the field as well.

These five pathologies – unilateral disdain, mutual animus, inadvertent omission, overt opposition, and boundary battles – may not exhaust the range of threats to the health of IPE today. But they clearly stand out in terms of both immediacy and intensity. "Here" is not a comfortable place for our field of study to be.

There

What about "There" – where we want to go? Our aim, fundamentally, should be to find appropriate remedies for each of the five pathologies. "There" can be defined by the basic course corrections that, arguably, are needed to counter these imminent threats. General principles to guide strategy have also been explored in preceding chapters. Two goals in particular may be deemed paramount.

One goal is to alleviate the problem of unilateral disdain, which regrettably limits IPE's contributions to public discourse. Chapter 3 urged doing whatever possible to elevate Counsel as a goal for the field as a whole. I know that many in the invisible college disagree, but for reasons spelled out in Chapter 3, I regard this as a priority. IPE has much to offer to policy debates in the public arena. Scholars with interests that extend beyond the ivory tower should be encouraged to communicate more effectively to decision makers and to shape research to make results more directly useful to policy elites.

The second goal, which appeared in various guises in Chapters 3–5, is to counter the noxious effects of the extreme balkanization that plagues IPE. The aim should be to maximize opportunities to enjoy the blessings of diversity. For the problem of mutual animus, Chapter 3 argued that the imperative is to learn to see through each other's eyes: to substitute an Open Door for the Stuck Door. For the problems of inadvertent omission and overt opposition, Chapter 4 advocated greater use of a research approach known as analytic eclecticism, which seeks to go "beyond paradigms" to look for hidden commonalities and connections among competing models. And for the problem of boundary battles, Chapter 5 advocated paying more attention to what issues other scholars are interested in, keeping an open mind to alternative priorities. All of these initiatives, in one way or another, would seek to limit the potential downsides of diversity, making IPE a more comfortable place to be.

Together, these two goals define what is needed to get IPE back on track.

REMEDIES

The second step is to spell out, in practical terms, how these two goals might be attained. The task is to fashion remedies that will directly target the field's most threatening pathologies.

Public Engagement

Begin with the first goal: encouraging greater public engagement. The challenge here is not new. Many scholars of International Relations (IR) and IPE have long complained about an intellectual culture that prizes theory above practice (Maliniak et al. 2020). Yet a bias in favor of more purely academic pursuits persists, reinforced by generations of socialization within discourse coalitions and what one source calls "practices of intellectual reproduction" (Biersteker 2009: 310). To overcome that entrenched bias, a higher priority for policy analysis should be promoted. Specific opportunities for reform measures might include faculty standards, editorial policies, and program support.

First, *faculty standards*. As a general rule, most institutions of higher learning conduct some kind of periodic assessment of faculty performance to help shape personnel decisions. Who deserves tenure or promotion? What salary increases seem warranted? In the University of California, where I taught for 30 years, these are called "merit reviews" and take place regularly at intervals of 2–4 years depending on rank. In principle such assessments are meant to take into consideration all of a candidate's professional activities, including policy engagement, during the period under review. In practice, however, everyone understands that more often than not it is formal scholarship that matters most – *primus inter pares*. What is needed is a radical revision of priorities, along lines suggested by Britain's Research Excellence Framework (REF) exercise, to give "impact" at least as much weight as more traditional academic activities – and to be serious about it. Assessment of the quality of policy-oriented work might not be easy, of course. How would we judge just where the line should be drawn between serious theory-driven analysis and pure political polemic? But that difficulty ought not be an excuse for not trying. Putting together well-conceived contributions to public discourse may be a challenge, but the effort should be loudly encouraged, not discouraged.

Second are *editorial policies*. Research journals also play a central role in setting standards for work in a field like IPE. Their preference, naturally, is to focus on new theoretical and empirical studies. But even in the most academic of IPE journals, it ought to be possible to make room as well for policy-oriented research that is practical, timely, and reasonably easy to read. During the many years I served on the board of editors of *International Organization* (a total of three decades in all), I repeatedly campaigned for the addition of a section dedicated solely to serious policy debate – regrettably, without success. My efforts were futile. Given the journal's absolute page limit, I was told, any new section would mean the sacrifice of an equivalent amount of fresh research. The trade-off was simply unacceptable. I disagreed, of course, and still do. Personally, I believe that one or two high-quality policy analyses per issue of any IPE journal would add more value than an equal number of marginal theoretical or empirical exercises. Currently, the *Review of International Political Economy* (*RIPE*) is unusual among major IPE journals in its willingness to add a commentary section from time to time when something of interest is available. (For an example, see Cohen 2012.) More journals should do the same.

Lastly comes *program support*. Conference programs effectively influence the direction of future scholarship by their decisions on what kind of work will be included or excluded. Funding sources do the same when they decide how to allocate scarce financial resources. In both cases – again along lines suggested by Britain's REF – deliberate efforts could be made to ensure that policy-relevant research receives its proper share of attention. At professional meetings, special roundtables could be organized to address key contemporary policy issues. In funding, more priority could be given to research proposals that include a commitment to wider dissemination of results in the public arena.

Diversity

The second goal is to moderate the less desirable side effects of diversity in IPE. As emphasized in earlier chapters, the problem is not diversity per se but rather what we choose to do with it. Our aim should be to make our differences a blessing, not a curse; cross-fertilization should be encouraged, not discouraged. We should read one another's work, participate in one another's meetings, and respectfully address one other's scholarship. The field's pluralism should be embraced, not denied.

How could cross-fertilization be promoted? Here it is possible to envision initiatives in at least four key dimensions of our field: instruction, scholarship, faculty appointments, and (again) editorial policies.

The first, *instruction*, would perhaps be the easiest. My suggestion is that everyone in IPE should be encouraged to expand class lectures and reading lists to include material from outside their own discourse coalition. As I noted back in Chapter 1, too often students are exposed to just a single version of what the field is about, solidifying fissures between factions. Instead, an all-out commitment should be made to acknowledge the legitimacy of alternative purposes. Instructors trained in an orthodox tradition should emphasize not just the virtues of positivism and empiricism, but also their limitations. Why *not* supplement objective analysis with normative criticism? Conversely, those coming from a more heterodox background should accept that to make the world a better place, it helps to know how its wheels and gears actually work. Why *not* supplement legitimate fault-finding with a bit of reductionist causal analysis? Our students deserve the whole truth.

In *scholarship*, my suggestion is that we all try our best to take into account the goals of perspectives other than our own. When writing a new book or journal article, we should make every effort to anticipate how our arguments might be received by related "networks and niches" in the field. If I emphasize positivist explanation, am I wrong to set aside more normative considerations? If I emphasize criticism of the status quo, am I neglecting the need for accurate empirical observation? If possible, we should submit our draft manuscripts to scholars of very different backgrounds to get a better sense of how our priorities may be seen through the eyes of others. Likewise, when we present research papers at conferences or other professional meetings, we should endeavor to line up discussants whose ideas of what IPE is about are very different from our own. Comprehension and Critique need not always be at sword's point.

Third, in *faculty appointments*, my suggestion is to encourage personnel diversity wherever and whenever possible. Of course, many college or university departments are too small to support an especially wide range of professional perspectives. For them, the only solution is to encourage closer relations with scholars in neighboring departments such as history, sociology, or anthropology. But where size allows, the aim should be to open faculty ranks as much as possible. We all know how, consciously or unconsciously, departments tend over time to become tribal, prioritizing certain types of hires over others. Choose a program and, more often than not, an informed academic will be able to tell you its general orientation. (I will resist the temptation to name names here.) We also know that newly minted PhDs, if they have a choice, naturally prefer to locate themselves where they are most likely to find colleagues with tastes similar to their own. Compartmentalization in the academic world is easy to understand but should be resisted.

Lastly, returning to *editorial policies*, my suggestion here is to urge more proactive efforts by journal editors to encourage work that goes beyond the narrow confines of a single research tradition. Editors often take the view that they are prisoners of the submission process. However much they may hunger for more diversity in their pages, they say, they can only select from among the manuscripts that are submitted for peer review. But that is a defeatist attitude. In fact, editors are in a unique position to identify questions that we ought to be thinking about. As I have argued elsewhere (Cohen 2010), there really is a good deal of room to exercise more ambitious initiative – for example, by actively soliciting review essays or surveys of selected issue areas, or by organizing symposia or special issues on selected themes. Some journals, such as *RIPE* and *International Studies Quarterly*, have already shown a willingness to move their editorial policies in that direction. Too many others, however, remain stubbornly resistant.

A MYSTERY

The third step is the hardest: to spell out a systematic plan of action to get us from Here to There – in other words, a winning strategy. It is not all that difficult to suggest what, in principle, might to be done to revitalize IPE. Anyone with even a passing familiarity with the field can dream up a list of potential remedies. But can dreams be translated into reality? Practical implementation is quite another matter.

One thing is for sure – the problem is not a lack of imagination. There is no dearth of good ideas. I am by no means alone in my dreams for a healthier IPE. Indeed, many of the sorts of remedies that I have suggested are familiar and have already been articulated in some form by others at one time or another. Reforms of editorial policies, for example, have been advocated by *inter alia* Robert Denemark (2010) and Nicola Phillips (2011), both veteran IPE journal editors. Likewise, problems with today's instructional norms have been highlighted by the likes of

Kathleen McNamara (2011) and Peter Katzenstein (2011). And the need to correct alleged prejudices in faculty standards has been emphasized by just about anyone who has ever been denied a job or tenure. The field hardly lacks for innovative thinking about where we could go from Here. Yet, in practice, we rarely get to There. The sad fact is that few prescriptions, however appealing, actually get implemented. On the contrary, systematic attempts over the years at serious reform have been few and far between. As has been noted by astute observers (e.g., Katzenstein 2011; Sharman 2011), a disconnect seems to prevail between what scholars say they want for our field and what they actually do. In the words of two senior US researchers, "The disconnect between the ways that scholars talk ... in private conversations, and the ways that they publicly present their own research or assess the research of others is sometimes rather startling" (Farrell and Finnemore 2011: 59). Though threats to the field's health are frequently invoked, action is rarely taken. Jason Sharman calls it a mystery:

> [Many scholars] call for greater dialogue, respect for diversity and bridge-building between different intellectual communities ... The mystery or paradox, however, is that if everyone is so much in favor of exchange, cross-fertilization, tolerance of diversity and so on, why do we have the sort of problems of intellectual isolationism and uninformed mutual disdain that most contributors identify? (Sharman 2011: 197)

That of course is the key question. *Why* is there such a disconnect? The answer, I submit, lies in power relations: the asymmetrical distribution of influence at the heart of our field of study. That seems the most realistic explanation; it certainly fits the facts. Like most social institutions, IPE's invisible college is distinctly hierarchical in structure. A limited number of actors enjoy a nearly unlimited capacity to set standards and define goals. Randall Germain (2011) calls it "disciplinary power." Katzenstein (2011) uses the term "professional power." Sharman (2011) prefers "structural power." Whatever the label, those who possess such power are quite likely to favor the status quo, since it is they who tend to be most closely identified with currently dominant (dare I say "hegemonic"?) themes. Resistance to change would be their natural posture; the familiar will be favored. Hence it should come as no surprise that most appeals for reform are stymied by inertia. Within discourse coalitions, each ensconced in its own silo, conformity to established norms is apt to be stubbornly defended. The mystery is in fact no mystery at all. The disconnect can be attributed first and foremost to the exercise of influence by those effectively in charge – those who play a major role as gatekeepers.

GATEKEEPERS

Generically, a gatekeeper is someone who controls access to something of importance, such as information or professional certification. In academia, gatekeepers play a dispositive role in framing answers to the Why, What, and How questions. They exercise major leverage over a discipline's choice of research perspectives and agendas – over what theoretical approaches will be regarded as "acceptable" and what subject matter may be seen as "appropriate." Most importantly, they determine what emerging ideas may be allowed to spread to a wider audience. Novel initiatives may be attractive in principle but will make little impact in practice unless gatekeepers open the door to let them in. The nature of gatekeeper power has been aptly summarized by Ben Clift, a British scholar, together with two colleagues:

> Academic gatekeepers in positions of disciplinary influence ... play important roles in maintaining these boundaries around the field, clarifying what constitutes its core, defining appropriate conduct within it, and delineating what falls outside its realm. Their capacity to define propriety concerning admissibility, conduct, borders and external relations is reflective of power structures within academic disciplines. These gatekeepers shape the field by deciding which authors and works constitute crucial parts of the canon, what "counts" ... and what does not. (Clift et al. 2021)

Who are IPE's gatekeepers? Who decides what "counts?" In analytical terms, little guidance is provided by the extant literature in our field. Some quarter-century ago, the US scholar Sylvia Maxfield (1997) addressed the role of central banks in developing countries as "gatekeepers of growth." More recently, a Canadian-based researcher analyzed the "gatekeeper power" of big retail firms like Walmart in managing their networks of domestic and foreign suppliers (van der Ven 2018). And in 2021 Clift and his colleagues skillfully explored the role that gatekeepers have played over time in determining how the field of IPE remembers its own history (Clift et al. 2021). But otherwise, discussion is thin. Most commentaries do little more than pause briefly to mention "gatekeeping practices" before moving on. Little detail is provided.

As a practical matter, however, identifying who "counts" is not particularly difficult. Virtually all academic specialties share the same kind of hierarchical authority structure, with five classes of actors perched at the top: These are: (1) instructors; (2) personnel committees; (3) funding sources; (4) program chairs; and (5) editors. In this respect once again, as I noted back at the outset, our field is by no means unique.

In effect, this quintet of gatekeepers traces the professional trajectory of a typical aspiring young scholar, from initial university training to the search for a job and ultimately promotion and tenure; then onward to financial support for research; and, finally, to the dissemination of research results in conference programs or other meetings and in journals or books. At the end of the process a seasoned instructor emerges, and the cycle begins all over again with the next generation of hopeful student wannabes. At each stage of an individual's advancement through the profession stand these actors who can make or break a career. None of these agents may think of themselves as playing a key gatekeeper role on behalf of an entire discipline like IPE; certainly no one appointed them to the part. Yet that is their impact, in our field as in others. Each of them is in a position to exercise significant authority over scholarly practices and trends.

Instructors

The central role of instructors in training future generations of IPE's invisible college has already been emphasized in Chapters 1 and 3 as well as earlier in this chapter. An ancient Chinese proverb says that "a journey of a thousand miles begins with a single step." By their choice of what to include in their lectures and reading lists, instructors largely determine the direction of that first step as well as the path for the journey beyond. As Katzenstein contends, "Through the training of graduate students ... many of us have a more direct effect on the field of IPE" (Katzenstein 2011: 110).

Ideally, from the start, students should be exposed to multiple versions of the field, to enable them eventually to make their own independent judgments. As I have suggested, they deserve the whole truth, not just a half-truth. In most instances, however, the tendency of instructors is to feed classes a monoculture in miniature, ignoring or discouraging other modes of thought. Critical theory is not very welcome in most US research departments. Mostly, it is dismissed as failing to meet the demanding standards of conventional social science. Conversely, young Americans with a background grounded in Open Economy Politics are confused if not wholly alienated by more heterodox approaches. Few

have a clue as to what is meant by "reproduction" or "commodification."
Even before students complete their training, gatekeeping has begun. As
Katzenstein laments:

> The elimination of pluralistic approaches to the subject of IPE in the seminars
> taught in the leading graduate programs ... bodes ill for the IPE field. When
> important intellectual issues touching on ontology, epistemology and theory
> are simply no longer taught, the next generation of scholar [*sic*] will no longer
> be aware of the choices and trade-offs we all confront in our research. And that
> makes reorientation and fresh starts more difficult in any field of scholarship.

Personnel Committees

Gatekeeping is also obviously involved when freshly minted PhDs go out
onto the job market, seeking a faculty appointment, and then again later
when it comes time to review the young hopeful's record for a tenure or
promotion decision. In some places, such as Britain, personnel decisions
are controlled centrally at the university level, lessening the risk of parochial or biased decisions by individual departments. Across most of the
world, however, the lead role in such instances is typically assigned to
a department committee mandated to come up with an informed recom-
mendation. Therein lies the problem.

In a perfect world, matters would be settled solely on the basis of
quality. Outcomes would be decided not by the candidate's choice of paradigm or problem, but rather by how well (or badly) her or his scholarship matches up with widely accepted professional standards. Objectivity
would rule. Sadly, however, that is not the real world. As a practical
matter, subjective elements are bound to creep into deliberations at the
department level, however much reviewers try to preserve the integrity
of the process. We arc all just human, after all. Does the candidate spend
too much time (or too little) on policy-oriented work? Does s/he seem
committed to the wrong research tradition? Does s/he publish in the
"right" journals? Is s/he on the opposite side of a boundary battle? Would
s/he "fit in" with the prevailing departmental ethos? Questions like these
may not be articulated explicitly, but there is little doubt that they lurk
implicitly, somewhere in the back of the minds of even the most assidu-
ous decision makers. Candidate careers hang in the balance.

Funding Sources

Funding sources come next. Even before a student completes her or his training, s/he is likely to have become acquainted with the arduous task of grant writing. Donors decide how scarce financial resources will be allocated. Whose research will be underwritten? As already noted, their answers go far to shape the agenda for future scholarship in the field.

Funding agencies include all kinds of institutional actors, from universities and foundations to think tanks and government agencies. With few exceptions, all tend to be quite explicit about their priorities. Some granting agencies favor work in a particular scholarly tradition; others, concurring with the British REF's stress on "impact," are eager to finance applied policy analysis; and yet others express a penchant for specific issues or selected geographic areas. Candidates, therefore, quickly learn that if they want to maximize their chances for support, they must be careful to tailor their applications more or less to donor preferences. Admittedly, the gatekeeping impact here is subtle. Aspiring scholars are by no means obligated to apply to any particular source – certainly not to any source with whose priorities they sharply disagree. But few new members of the invisible college, after years of foregone income and accumulating debt, are likely to be in a position to be choosy. Generally penurious, they may not feel that they have much alternative. Again, careers hang in the balance.

Program Chairs

Whether underwritten or not, research must seek an outlet if it is to make an impact. For most novice scholars, the most immediate opportunities for dissemination are to be found in the programs of conferences and other professional meetings where a freshly written paper can be presented to an audience. Conference programs also go far to shape the agenda for future scholarship. They offer opportunities to test the quality of a candidate's work through exposure to discussion and criticism by peers. They also help candidates to begin building personal networks of colleagues with similar research interests. The challenge, however, is getting on a program in the first place – a hurdle that is not so easy to clear.

Customarily, the question of whose research will be featured at conferences or other meetings typically falls into the hands of program chairs. Their answers, clearly, may also help to shape the agenda for future scholarship in the field. Program chairs enjoy absolute veto power. Anyone can propose a paper for presentation, but it is program chairs who deliver the verdict. Here too, in principle, matters should be settled objectively on the basis of quality alone. Does a proposed paper appear to meet accepted professional standards? But here too, in practice, elements of subjectivity are quite apt to creep into the process. Decisions about what will be included or excluded today are very likely to have an impact on career choices tomorrow.

Journal and Book Editors

The story is also much the same with journal and book editors. Nothing is more important to the dissemination of a young scholar's research than publication in some printed or digital form – the more highly rated, the better. But as we all know, that too is a difficult hurdle to clear. The process of editorial screening is arduous. New papers or book manuscripts can be submitted anywhere, of course. But like program chairs, editors also enjoy absolute veto power and acceptance rates are low. Nothing better illustrates the meaning of gatekeeping than a rejection letter from an editor. To avoid rejection, candidates will undertake whatever revisions seem needed to meet an editor's expectations. Cumulatively, that too will go far to shape practices and trends in our field of study. As Phillips summarizes, "the practice of editorial screening, or what some like to call 'gate keeping' ... deciding what is or is not appropriate and acceptable scholarship, is at least as important as wider intellectual trends, and indeed may well be a crucial *cause* of their emergence" (Phillips 2011: 75–6; emphasis in the original).

THE BIG CHALLENGE

The Big Challenge, then, is clear. IPE is plagued by a variety of pathologies. Remedies to revitalize the field may be conceived but are stymied by powerful gatekeepers. To get the field back on track, a concrete plan of action is required. What might a winning strategy look like?

To begin, a winning strategy requires *leaders* – actors prepared to pave the way, making the necessary effort to change minds. Reforms do not materialize from thin air. We cannot simply wait for something akin to spontaneous combustion to fire up the process. In a group like IPE's invisible college, decision making can be expected to be interdependent: the behavior of any one individual will depend, at least in part, on what behavior is anticipated from others. Hence new initiatives in general tend to be discouraged by inertial network effects. Few individuals are willing to risk committing to fresh norms unless others can be counted upon to do the same. But since others are likely to feel the same way, the most probable outcome is a cautious retreat to the status quo. Without determined, proactive leadership, therefore, even the most attractive ideas for change may be fated to remain little more than fantasies, hardly worth the paper (or computer screen) they are written on.

Where will the needed leadership come from? In analytical terms, we are faced with the classic problem of collective action first formally articulated by the US scholar Mancur Olson in his memorable book *The Logic of Collective Action* (Olson 1965). Just because some group has interests in common, Olson demonstrated, there is no reason to expect that its membership will necessarily band together to promote them. At issue are the costs of any reform initiative. Change may be promoted by selected actors, but only if the gains to them from their efforts can be expected to exceed the costs that they themselves might have to bear. Those actors are known as a "privileged group." They are privileged because they can benefit from collective action on a net basis even if they pay a disproportionate share of the costs.

The dilemma is that in IPE it is difficult to find a privileged group (in the Olsonian sense). Logic would seem to suggest that we look for candidates among those in the field with the greatest disciplinary power. Those of course would be IPE's gatekeepers. But for those actors, as already noted, resistance to change – not reform – would be their natural posture. The field's gatekeepers may be stubborn, but they are not irrational. By all appearances, they simply do not feel that their interests would be best served by taking a leadership role in any major reform initiative. If pro-change leaders are to be found, we have to look elsewhere.

The best place to look, I submit, would be among the assorted professional bodies that have emerged over the years as an integral part of the ecology of IPE. As noted back in Chapter 1, organized IPE-related societies have sprung up across the globe, each intended to promote networking and debate in the invisible college. These range from Britain's long-standing International Political Economy Group and the IPE Section of America's International Studies Association (ISA) to smaller and newer groups in Australia, Canada, Continental Europe, Latin America, and even Turkey and China. Ostensibly, all are dedicated to serving the best interests of our field of study. It would seem natural, therefore, to look to them for help in getting IPE back on track.

Admittedly, learned societies may not be perfect for the role. As any student of organizational behavior would be quick to remind us, voluntary associations often find themselves "captured" by an activist minority determined to promote ideas that may not be shared by a more passive majority. The risk, however, is apt to be moderate when it comes to assemblies of academics, who are more likely than most mortals to be keenly alert to any lack of proper representation. In any event, who else is there? The perfect should not be the enemy of the good. If there are any actors that might conceivably be capable of countervailing the disciplinary power of the field's multiple gatekeepers, it would be IPE's several professional bodies.

A PLAN OF ACTION

What can associations do? I do not claim that they can be miracle-workers. At a minimum, though, a two-part plan of action does seem to me to be feasible. First would be agreement on what I would call a Code of Best Practices. Second would be a set of creative measures designed to promote adoption of the Code's principles in everyday use.

Code of Best Practices

The Code of Best Practices would promulgate new (or newly articulated) standards for the field. The idea would be to agree on a common set of remedies for IPE's most pressing pathologies – what may be regarded as best practices for the field as a whole. Ideally, to maximize impact, the Code would be negotiated and endorsed collectively by as many of IPE's professional bodies as possible. But even if a broad consensus proves elusive, progress need not be delayed. Negotiations could be started by a smaller number of societies, with the resulting accord then left "open" for others to sign onto at their own pace.

The Code would begin by affirming the two goals that I have high-lighted: to encourage both greater public engagement in IPE scholarship and more active cross-fertilization among the field's diverse "networks and niches." For the first goal, a higher priority for policy analysis should be agreed. For the second, more emphasis should be placed on the value to be gained from the field's pluralism. The remainder of the Code would then spell out in concrete terms what needs to be done to promote each goal in practice, along the lines suggested in this chapter. Instructors should be encouraged to do more to expose students to the full range of diversity in the field. Faculty assessments should place more emphasis on public engagement and diversification of personnel. Funding sources and program chairs should offer an open door to all research traditions and theoretical perspectives. And journal editors should be pushed to make more room in their pages for policy debates and invited surveys and symposia. Consideration might even be given to the possibility of creating new high-quality journals that like *Foreign Affairs* and *International Affairs* would deliberately target an audience of policy elites.

The second part of the plan would then put the Code of Best Practices to work. Here, caution would not necessarily be a virtue. On the contrary, if we are to successfully challenge ingrained habits, we need to be prepared to make waves. We must not be afraid to think outside the box. Our prescriptions must be as imaginative as IPE's pathologies appear to demand. Nothing should be rejected simply because it is unusual or as yet untested.

The targets would be IPE's gatekeepers, whose resistance to change must be attacked aggressively if real reform is to occur. Gatekeepers are the lead actors in this drama. For example, why not start with instructors at the start of a young scholar's career trajectory? Associations could encourage greater pluralism in teaching by sponsoring the systematic compilation of bibliographies representing most if not all of the major theoretical perspectives in the field. Many instructors may be open to including unfamiliar material in their courses but simply do not know where to begin. To be effective, such lists would have to be edited carefully and updated regularly with easy access assured through the internet. It might even be possible to create a public repository where course syllabi could be stored and made available to anyone looking to widen the scope of their courses.

But how can gatekeepers be persuaded to alter their behavior? Professional associations obviously lack the capacity to directly dictate to instructors or others with disciplinary power. Societies as such can neither coerce nor bribe. Nonetheless, they are not without options to exercise some degree of influence. Both sticks and carrots are available. The key lies in the structure of incentives that motivate gatekeeping practices. A fair assumption is that gatekeepers care about their reputation. As much as anyone, they crave respect and dread reproach. That gives professional associations leverage. Learned societies may lack the means to exercise formal authority in the field. But informally it is within their power to apply leverage by offering gatekeepers either approbation or opprobrium as circumstances seem to warrant. Implemented carefully, that leverage could go a long way toward achieving the two goals of the Code.

Sticks

The biggest stick that associations might wield would be some kind of platform for publicly evaluating gatekeeper behavior. A possible model is offered in Britain, where universities have already gone far to open up the instruction function by formally promoting student participation in decisions about course modules. Students are rightly seen as the constituency with the greatest direct interest in quality teaching. They are even given the opportunity to devise "shadow" curricula for comparative purposes. Associations in other nations could actively push for similar arrangements in their own educational institutions.

Alternatively, the aim might be to create a venue where scholars as well as students could regularly rate instructors, editors, and others with disciplinary power in the field. It would not be necessary to go so far as to create a public "blacklist" for all to see. That might be seen as too provocative – a bridge too far. More likely, it would be enough just to offer members of the invisible college a chance to "name and shame" any recalcitrant practices. It is a safe bet that gatekeeper resistance to change might be eroded significantly by a slew of poor ratings.

In the age of the internet, constructing a venue like that would not be difficult. Here a possible model is provided by the website Rate My Professors (RMP), which freely allows students in the United States, Canada, and Britain to assign ratings to both instructors and campuses. I myself have frequently consulted the RMP site to see what I might need to do to improve my teaching. (My greatest regret is that I never was awarded a red chili pepper, which signifies which professors are considered "hot.") Something similar could be created by a consortium of IPE associations and then advertised widely to their memberships. Given the widespread discontent that I have detected in private correspondence with friends and colleagues in the field, I would not be surprised to see such a site receive a warm welcome. At last, the invisible college would have a formal outlet for its frustrations.

Carrots

Conversely, the biggest carrot that associations might offer would be some kind of official recognition for behavior that conforms most closely with the Code of Best Practices. Here the intent would be not to "name and shame" but to "honor and esteem." The idea would be to accord special respect to instructors, editors, or others who really endeavor to help remedy what ails the field. Even whole departments or programs could be singled out for praise for their personnel policies. This would be not a blacklist but an honors list. Another safe bet is that at least some amelioration of gatekeeper behavior would be prompted by the prospect of an improved reputation.

Here too, implementation would not be difficult. One possibility might be to establish a ranking system for collective actors – such as departments, journals, or book publishers – that could be based on metrics established by the Code of Best Practices. Alternatively (or additionally) new awards could be created intended specifically to recognize the efforts of individuals. Our field is already littered with awards for all sorts of high achievement in scholarship – from "best" this or that (best book, best journal article, best conference paper, and so on) to honors for mentoring or lifetime professional achievement. But apart from the Outstanding Activist Scholar Award of the ISA's IPE section, which formally acknowledges work in the public sphere, few awards are offered for activity that specifically targets either of the two goals that I have emphasized. So why not a new award for instructors, program chairs, or editors who best promote an appreciation of IPE's many "networks and niches?" One can quibble about how truly meaningful awards of any kind may be. For some scholars, awards seem to be little more than a crap shoot; others fear that they are prone to corruption as a result of covert politicking or personal biases. Yet it is hard to argue that, on balance, they do more harm than good. For many beginners in the field, struggling to make a name for themselves, awards are a true incentive.

CONCLUSION

My conclusion, therefore, is actually a bit optimistic. Despite all the pathologies threatening our field of study, IPE *can* get its groove back. It won't be easy. Problems like unilateral disdain, mutual animosity, inadvertent omission, overt opposition, and boundary battles are complex and deep-rooted; and the power of gatekeepers to resist significant change is considerable. Yet room for revitalization does exist if the will is there. As I said at the outset, our specialty has seemingly switched to autopilot, drifting aimlessly off course. The aim of this book has been to provide a needed wake-up call. My message is plain. We need to get started. It is

not too late to get the field back on track. International Political Economy
has not passed its peak – not yet.

REFERENCES

Biersteker, Thomas J. (2009), "The Parochialism of Hegemony: Challenges
for 'American' International Relations," in Arlene B. Tickner and Ole
Waever, eds., *International Relations Scholarship Around the World* (London:
Routledge), 308–27.
Clift, Ben, Peter M. Kristensen, and Ben Rosamond (2021), "Remembering
and Forgetting IPE: Disciplinary History as Boundary Work," *Review of
International Political Economy* (forthcoming).
Cohen, Benjamin J. (2010), "Are IPE Journals Becoming Boring?" *International
Studies Quarterly* 54:3, 887–91.
Cohen, Benjamin J. (2012), "The Future of the Euro: Let's Get Real," *Review of
International Political Economy* 19:4, 689–700.
Denemark, Robert A. (2010), "Toward a Vibrant IPE Literature: Commiserating
with Cohen," *International Studies Quarterly* 54:3, 897–9.
Farrell, Henry and Martha Finnemore (2011), "Ontology, Methodology, and
Causation in the American School of International Political Economy,"
in Nicola Phillips and Catherine E. Weaver, eds., *International Political
Economy: Debating the Past, Present and Future* (London: Routledge),
53–63.
Germain, Randall D. (2011), "The 'American' School of IPE? A Dissenting
View," in Nicola Phillips and Catherine E. Weaver, eds., *International Political
Economy: Debating the Past, Present and Future* (London: Routledge), 83–91.
Katzenstein, Peter J. (2011), "Mid-Atlantic: Sitting on the Knife's Sharp Edge,"
in Nicola Phillips and Catherine E. Weaver, eds., *International Political
Economy: Debating the Past, Present and Future* (London: Routledge),
105–15.
Maliniak, Daniel, Susan Peterson, Ryan Powers, and Michael J. Tierney, eds.
(2020), *Bridging the Theory–Practice Divide in International Relations*
(Washington, DC: Georgetown University Press).
Maxfield, Sylvia (1997), *Gatekeepers of Growth: The International Political
Economy of Central Banking in Developing Countries* (Princeton, NJ:
Princeton University Press).
McNamara, Kathleen (2011), "Of Intellectual Monocultures and the Study of
IPE," in Nicola Phillips and Catherine E. Weaver, eds., *International Political
Economy: Debating the Past, Present and Future* (London: Routledge),
64–73.
Olson, Mancur (1965), *The Logic of Collective Action: Public Goods and the
Theory of Groups* (Cambridge, MA: Harvard University Press).
Phillips, Nicola (2011), "The Slow Death of Pluralism," in Nicola Phillips and
Catherine E. Weaver, eds., *International Political Economy: Debating the
Past, Present and Future* (London: Routledge), 74–82.
Sharman, Jason C. (2011), "Mantras, Bridges and Benchmarks: Assessing
the Future of IPE," in Nicola Phillips and Catherine E. Weaver, eds.,

International Political Economy: Debating the Past, Present and Future (London: Routledge), 197–202.

van der Ven, Hamish (2018), "Gatekeeper Power: Understanding the Influence of Lead Firms over Transnational Sustainability Standards," *Review of International Political Economy* 25:5, 624–46.

Appendices

APPENDIX A: PRINCIPAL THEORETICAL APPROACHES TO IPE

Orthodox perspectives	Heterodox perspectives
These approaches share a preference for a state-centric ontology, positivism, closed disciplinary boundaries, and rigorous methodology.	These approaches, by contrast, are less state-centric; agendas are broader and more normative; boundaries are more open; and methodology is less formal.
Variants	Variants
Liberalism assumes that economics dominates politics and is more comfortable with a domestic level of analysis focusing on policy processes.	**System-level theories** center on global structures and processes. Examples include classical Marxism, dependency, world-systems theory, and world orders.
Realism assumes that politics dominates economics and favors a systemic level of analysis focusing on state power and interests.	**Critical theory** challenges orthodoxy of every sort and is highly normative, with a focus on dominance and inequality.
Constructivism focuses on the role of ideas and social norms, emphasizing a logic of appropriateness rather than a logic of consequence.	**Extensions** seek to expand the boundaries of the field by adding an emphasis on some allegedly missing element such as history, non-elite actors, culture, gender, or complexity.

APPENDIX B: THE ANGLOPHONE SURVEY

Abdelal, Rawi, Mark Blyth, and Craig Parsons, eds. (2010), *Constructing the International Economy* (Ithaca, NY: Cornell University Press).

Anderson, Greg and Christopher Kukucha, eds. (2015), *International Political Economy* (Oxford and New York: Oxford University Press).

Ardalan, Kavous (2018), *Global Political Economy: A Multi-paradigmatic Approach* (Cham, Switzerland: Springer International Publishing).

Balaam, David N. and Bradford Dillman (2019), *Introduction to International Political Economy*, 7th edition (New York: Routledge).

Blyth, Mark, ed. (2009), *Routledge Handbook of International Political Economy (IPE): IPE as a Global Conversation* (London and New York: Routledge).

Cafruny, Alan W., Leila Simona Talani, and Gonzalo Pozo Martin, eds. (2016), *The Palgrave Handbook of Critical International Political Economy* (London: Palgrave Macmillan).

Cameron, Angus, Anastasia Nesvetailova, and Ronen Palan, eds. (2008), *International Political Economy*, 5 volumes (Los Angeles, London, New Delhi, and Singapore: Sage Publications).

Cohn, Theodore H. (2016), *Global Political Economy: Theory and Practice*, 7th edition (New York and London: Routledge).

Frieden, Jeffrey A., David A. Lake, and J. Lawrence Broz, eds. (2017), *International Political Economy: Perspectives on Global Power and Wealth*, 6th edition (New York and London: Norton).

Goddard, C. Roe, Patrick Cronin, and Kishor C. Dash, eds. (2003), *International Political Economy: State–Market Relations in a Changing Global Order*, 2nd edition (Boulder, CO: Lynne Rienner).

Hobson, John M. and Leonard Seabrooke, eds. (2007), *Everyday Politics of the World Economy* (Cambridge and New York: Cambridge University Press).

Hülsemeyer, Axel (2010), *International Political Economy: A Reader* (Oxford and New York: Oxford University Press).

Lairson, Thomas D. and David Skidmore (2017), *International Political Economy: The Struggle for Power and Wealth in a Globalizing World* (New York and London: Routledge).

Maswood, Javed S. (2008), *International Political Economy and Globalization*, 2nd edition (Singapore, Hackensack, NJ, and London: World Scientific).

Miller, Raymond C. (2018) *International Political Economy: Contrasting World Views*, 2nd edition (New York and London: Routledge).

Oatley, Thomas, H., ed. (2010), *Debates in International Political Economy* (London: Longman Pearson).

Oatley, Thomas H. (2018), *International Political Economy*, 6th edition (New York and London: Routledge).

O'Brien, Robert and Marc Williams (2016), *Global Political Economy: Evolution and Dynamics*, 5th edition (London and New York: Palgrave Macmillan).

Palan, Ronen, ed. (2013), *Global Political Economy: Contemporary Theories*, 2nd edition (London and New York: Routledge).

Paquin, Stéphane (2016), *Theories of International Political Economy: An Introduction* (Ontario, Canada: Oxford University Press).

Paul, Darel E. and Abla Amawi, eds. (2013), *The Theoretical Evolution of International Political Economy: A Reader*, 3rd edition (Oxford and New York: Oxford University Press).

Pettman, Ralph, ed. (2012), *Handbook on International Political Economy* (Singapore: World Scientific).

Phillips, Nicola, ed. (2005), *Globalizing the International Political Economy* (London and New York: Palgrave Macmillan).

Phillips, Nicola and Catherine Weaver, eds. (2011), *International Political Economy: Debating the Past, Present and Future* (New York and London: Routledge).

Ravenhill, John, ed. (2017), *Global Political Economy*, 5th edition (New York: Oxford University Press).

Reisman, David (2019), *Global Political Economy: Beyond the Nation State* (Cheltenham, UK and Northampton, MA, USA: Edward Elgar Publishing).

Shaw, Timothy M., Laura C. Mahrenbach, Renu Modi, and Xu Yi-Chong, eds. (2019), *The Palgrave Handbook of Contemporary International Political Economy* (London: Palgrave Macmillan).

Shields, Stuart, Ian Bruff, and Huw Macartney, eds. (2011), *Critical International Political Economy: Dialogue, Debate, and Dissensus* (London and New York: Palgrave Macmillan).

Smith, Roy, Imad El-Anis, and Christopher Farrands (2017), *International Political Economy in the 21st Century: Contemporary Issues and Analyses*, 2nd edition (London and New York: Routledge).

Sobel, Andrew (2013), *International Political Economy in Context: Individual Choices, Global Effects* (Thousand Oaks, CA: CQ Press).

Spero, Joan Edelman and Jeffrey A. Hart (2010), *The Politics of International Economic Relations*, 7th edition (Boston: Cengage Learning).

Stubbs, Richard and Geoffrey R.D. Underhill, eds. (2006), *Political Economy and the Changing Global Order*, 3rd edition (Toronto, Oxford, and New York: Oxford University Press).

Walter, Andrew and Gautam Sen (2009), *Analyzing the Global Political Economy* (Princeton, NJ: Princeton University Press).

Watson, Matthew (2005), *Foundations of International Political Economy* (New York: Palgrave Macmillan).

Weisband, Edward and Courtney I.P. Thomas (2010), *International Political Economy: Navigating the Logic Streams: An Introduction* (Dubuque, IA: Kendall Hunt).

APPENDIX C: THE LEFT-OUT SURVEY

Bell, Stephen and Hui Feng (2019), "Policy Diffusion as Empowerment: Domestic Agency and the Institutional Dynamics of Monetary Policy Diffusion in China," *Globalizations* 16:6, 919–33.

Bieler, Andreas and Chun-Yi Lee (2017), "Chinese Labour in the Global Economy: An Introduction," *Globalizations* 14:2, 179–88.

Glaze, Simon (2015), "Schools Out: Adam Smith and Pre-disciplinary International Political Economy," *New Political Economy* 20:5, 679–701.

Gonzalez, Carlos (2019), "Is the Locus of Class Development of the Transnational Capitalist Class Situated within Nation-states or in the Emergent Transnational Space?" *Global Network: A Journal of Transnational Affairs* 19:2, 261–79.

Harris, Kevin and Brendan McQuade (2015), "Notes on the Method of World-System Biography," *Journal of World-Systems Research* 21:2, 276–86.

Mahutga, Mathew C. (2014), "Global Production Networks and International Inequality: Making a Case for a Meso-level Turn in Macro-Comparative Sociology," *Journal of World-Systems Research* 20:1, 11–37.

Mayer, Frederick W., Nicola Phillips, and Anne C. Posthuma (2017), "The Political Economy of Governance in a 'Global Value Chain World,'" *New Political Economy* 22:2, 129–33.

Mckeown, Anthony and John Glenn (2018), "The Rise of Resilience after the Financial Crises: A Case of Neoliberalism Rebooted?" *Review of International Studies* 44:2, 193–214.

Phillips, Nicola (2016), "Labour in Global Production: Reflections on Coxian Insights in a World of Global Value Chains," *Globalizations* 13:5, 594–607.

Robinson, William I. and Jeb Sprague (2018), "The Transnational Capitalist Class," in Mark Juergensmeyer, Mafred B. Steger, and Saskia Sassen, eds., *Handbook of Global Studies* (Oxford: Oxford University Press).

Stengel, Frank and Dirk Nabers (2019), "Symposium: The Contribution of Laclau's Discourse Theory to International Relations and International Political Economy," *New Political Science* 41:2, 248–62.

Wullweber, Joscha (2019), "Money, State, Hegemony: A Political Ontology of Money," *New Political Science* 41:2, 313–28.

APPENDIX D: THE EUROPEAN SURVEY

Bana, Cornel and Daniela Gabor (2016), "The Political Economy of Shadow Banking," *Review of International Political Economy* 23:6, 901–14.

Baroncelli, Eugenia (2015), "Mind the Gap: IR and the Challenge of International Politics," *Rivista Italiana di Scienza Politica* 45:1, 79–101.

Bayliss, Kate, Ben Fine, and Mary Robertson (2017), "Introduction to Special Issue on the Material Cultures of Financialisation," *New Political Economy* 22:4, 355–70.

Bernards, Nick and Malcolm Campbell-Verduyn (2014), "Understanding Technological Change in Global Finance Through Infrastructures," *Review of International Political Economy* 21:5, 773–89.

Bieling, Hans-Jürgen, Tobias Haas, and Julia Lux (2014), "Introduction: The Development and Perspectives of International Political Economy (IPE) after the World Financial Crisis," *Zeitschrift für Außen- und Sicherheitspolitik* 6:1, 1–10.

Cahill, Damien and Alfredo Saad-Filho (2017), "Neoliberalism Since the Crisis," *Critical Sociology* 43:4–5, 611–13.

Dannreuther, Charlie, Scott Lavery, and Lucia Quaglia (2019), "Brexit and the 'Reproduction' of British Capitalism," *New Political Economy* 24:3, 404–7.

Farrell, Henry and Abraham Newman (2016), "The New Interdependence Approach: Theoretical Development and Empirical Demonstration," *Review of International Political Economy* 23:5, 713–36.

Grabel, Ilene and Kevin P. Gallagher (2015), "Capital Controls and the Global Financial Crisis: An Introduction," *Review of International Political Economy* 22:1, 1–6.

Green, Jeremy and Colin Hay (2015), "Towards a New Political Economy of the Crisis: Getting What Went Wrong Right," *New Political Economy* 20:3, 331–41.

Hameiri, Shahar and Lee Jones (2015), "Probing the Links Between Political Economy and Non-Traditional Security: Themes, Approaches and Instruments," *International Politics* 54:4, 371–88.

Jensen, Nathan M., Bumba Mukherjee, and William T. Bernhard (2014), "Introduction: Survey and Experimental Research in International Political Economy," *International Interactions* 40:3, 287–304.

Koddenbrock, Kai (2018), "Structural Change of Globalization? Brexit, Trump(ism), China's Strategies, and the Political Economy of International Relations. Introduction to the Forum," *Zeitschrift für Internationale Beziehungen* 25:2, 126–43. [Original in German]

Kranke, Matthias (2014), "Which 'C' Are You Talking About? Critical Meets Cultural IPE," *Millennium* 42:3, 897–907.

Kuzemko, Caroline, Andrew Lawrence, and Matthew Watson (2019), "New Directions in the International Political Economy of Energy," *Review of International Political Economy* 26:1, 1–24.

Lavery, Scott, Lucia Quaglia, and Charlie Dannreuther (2019), "Brexit and the International Orientation of British Capitalism," *New Political Economy* 24:2, 252–7.

Robinson, William I. (2016), "Introduction: Race in the Capitalist World-System," *Journal of World-Systems Research* 22:1, 3–8.

Snider, Erin A. (2017), "International Political Economy and the New Middle East," *PS: Political Science & Politics* 50:3, 646–67.

APPENDIX E: THE LATIN AMERICAN SURVEY

Chagas-Bastos, Fabricio H. (2018), "The Invention of the International Insertion: Intellectual Foundations and Conceptual Historical Evolution," *Análisis Político* 31:94, 10–30. [Original in Spanish]

Clemente, Dario (2018), "Ruy Mauro Marini's Contributions to International Studies from Latin America," *Análisis Político* 31:94, 75–92. [Original in Spanish]

Deciancio, Melisa (2018), "International Political Economy in the Discipline of International Relations in Argentina," *Desafíos* 30:2, 15–42. [Original in Spanish]

Jimenez-Peña, Gabriel, Ralf J. Leiteritz, and Carolina Urrego-Sandoval (2018), "Dossier: 'State of the Art of Latin American International Political Economy,'" *Revista Desafíos* 30:2, 9–12. [Original in Spanish]

Lechini, Gladys and Patricia Rojo (2019), "The Contributions of 'the School of Rosario' to the Study of International Relations in Argentina," *Revista de Relaciones Internacionales de la UNAM* 133, 185–205. [Original in Spanish]

Madariaga, Aldo (2019), "The Resurgence of Political Economy in Today's Political Science," *Revista de Economía Institucional* 21:41, 21–50. [Original in Spanish]

Peixoto Batista, Juliana (2017), "IPE and International Relations: Where is the Law?" *Relaciones Internacionales* 26:53, 181–94. [Original in Spanish]

Ramos, Leonardo and Marina Scotelaro (2018), "The State of the Art of International Political Economy of Brazil: Possibilities to Think (and Practice) an IPE from Below," *Desafíos* 30:2, 127–57. [Original in Spanish]

Tussie, Diana (2015), "International Relations and International Political Economy: Notes for the Debate," *Relaciones Internacionales* 24:48, 155–75. [Original in Spanish]

Tussie, Diana and Pia Riggirozzi (2015), "A Global Conversation: Rethinking IPE in Post-hegemonic Scenarios," *Contexto Internacional* 37:3, 1041–68.

Zelicovich, Julieta (2018), "What Matters is the Question. Contributions of International Political Economy in Latin America, for the Debate in the Context of the Crisis of Globalization," *Relaciones Internacionales* 27:54, 55–68. [Original in Spanish]

Index